A Year
of Garden
Bees and
Bugs

First published in the United Kingdom in 2024 by
Batsford
43 Great Ormond Street
London WC1N 3HZ
An imprint of B.T. Batsford Holdings Ltd

Copyright © B.T. Batsford Ltd, 2024
Text copyright © Dominic Couzens & Gail Ashton, 2024
Illustrations by Lesley Buckingham
Entomological Consultant: Rory Dimond

ISBN: 9781849947954

A CIP catalogue record for this book is available from the British Library.

30 29 28 27 26 25 24 23
10 9 8 7 6 5 4 3 2 1

Reproduction by Rival Colour Ltd, UK
Printed and bound by Toppan Leefung Ltd, China

This book can be ordered direct from the publisher at
www.batsfordbooks.com, or try your local bookshop.

MIX
Paper | Supporting
responsible forestry
FSC
www.fsc.org
FSC® C104723

A Year of Garden Bees and Bugs

Dominic Couzens & Gail Ashton

BATSFORD

Contents

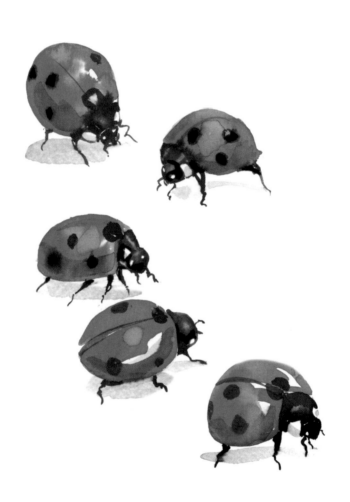

Introduction

F OR THOSE OF US WHO LOVE THE NATURAL WORLD, the passage of the year can be joyfully measured by the appearance of different animals, plants and fungi. In the temperate world, where seasons are extreme, the first swallow of spring or the first flush of spring flowers can lift the heart, while a flock of geese flying high overhead may presage autumn and the thick coat of a squirrel is a sign of winter to come. In the tropics, seasons are defined more by the rains, and there is often the same burst of bird song and fruiting trees in the wake of a downpour. The ebb and flow of the living world throughout the year is as certain as the turning of the tides, the rising of the moon and the setting of the sun.

What many enthusiasts don't realize, though, is that the passage of the year can also be defined by the appearance of invertebrates – animals without backbones, but often with multiple legs and sometimes with none; that's bees, flies, worms, woodlice and spiders, to name a few. Most of us recognize that butterflies are seasonal, and that bees are commoner in the summer than the winter. But not everybody realizes that different sorts of butterflies, and different sorts of beetles and flies and bees and wasps, make their appearance in such a way that you could order your seasonal clock by them. For example, a temperate garden will see a succession of bees, with a flush of mining bees in the spring, carpenter bees in the summer and ivy bees in the autumn. Beetles are the same – in the UK we have oil beetles in spring, cockchafers in May and common red soldier beetles in July. The gloriously shiny Christmas beetle appears in parts of Australia at – yes, you guessed it – Christmas, felicitously resembling a tree ornament. In temperate regions, we even have special seasonal insect events – flying ant day in the UK, usually in July, and in the US the periodical cicadas in late spring and dog-day cicadas in high summer.

It isn't just the sight of invertebrates that sparks our imaginations; there are sounds at certain times of the year that are simply quintessential to the passage of the seasons. The low, dense hum of a queen bumblebee rumbling into earshot, a crescendo that announces her inaugural flight to find food and set up home, kick-starts our sensory journey into spring. The pianissimo chirruping of crickets after dark, and the furtive stridulations of amorous grasshoppers in dry, sun-baked meadows are the sultry soundtrack of high summer. Then there is the almost imperceptible crinkling of an adult dragonfly emerging from its exuvia into the sunshine on a warm still morning, or the muffled, glassy clunk of a moth colliding with the outside light. There is a comforting familiarity to the almost continual, soft hum of a multitude of invertebrates, all keeping the world ticking happily over.

Globally, we are incredibly lucky to be able to share many insects across land masses. A sudden swelling of insect numbers at certain points in the year, marks the end of myriad transcontinental epic migratory journeys, whether it be the flamboyant procession of the monarch butterfly (see page 160) or the unassuming appearance of millions of hoverflies, so quiet that we hardly notice their appearance. It's difficult to comprehend how such small, delicate creatures can undertake some of the planet's most epic voyages, breaking many records along the way, but that they do, and the arrival of the marmalade hoverfly, for example, in our gardens in the UK can be equally as exciting as the screaming of the first swift above our heads.

Why the sudden commotion in spring? Like most animals, invertebrates exploit a window of opportunity to feed and reproduce, and that open window is never wider than during the warmest months, when daylight hours are in plentiful supply. Plants send forth new growth in the form of leaves and flowers, providing a glut of food resources for phytophagous (plant-eating) organisms. This in turn lures out the zoophages (carnivores), and thus the food web spans out into a complex network of feeding and hunting interactions in the soil, plants, and trees in our gardens. The end of winter heralds more than just a change in behaviour for many invertebrates. Lots of insects undergo a major transformation, revealing themselves to the spring sunshine in very different guises; having spent the winter as pudgy, hungry larvae under the ground or in rotting wood, they become armoured, winged adults. A few, even hardier, sorts can remain active throughout even the coldest conditions and take their own places in the invertebrate calendar. Snow fleas (Boreidae), for example, only come out in the coldest months, (flying in the face of the general rule that insects are beasts of summer) and are most visible against a backdrop of crisp, white snow.

Those warmth-seeking invertebrates that are tough enough to survive the winter haven't been far away either. They have hunkered down in sheltered nooks and crannies, their metabolisms slowed down to the point of basic life-support, known as diapause – the invertebrate version of hibernation. The first beams of warm sunlight trigger behaviour on a monumental scale, acting as a catalyst for the emergence of millions of tiny organisms. These organisms, in fulfilling their reproductive destinies, circumstantially perform essential ecosystem services on the side, such as pollination, recycling, fertilization and terraforming, without all of which our beautiful planet Earth would be uninhabitable.

The rewards of sharing our space with invertebrates are manifest. They can be seen in the pollinated flowers that bear fruit; in the soil structure that they engineer, which produces healthy plants, captures carbon and mitigates flooding; in the birds and mammals that eat them and feed them to their growing young; in the honey that sweetens our food; and in the astonishing array of natural pest control services that far surpass the abilities of modern pesticides. With this in mind, wouldn't it be lovely for us all to embrace their seasonal return and proclaim their arrival in our gardens? For they are, indeed, the little things that make the world go round.

So, the invertebrate year is just as thrilling as the changing bird year, or as the yearly march of flowering trees and herbs. In some ways, it is even more satisfying, because you usually don't need to travel to see it. There is perhaps no better way to appreciate the passage of the seasons than in your own garden. A temperate garden might only have visits from 20–30 species of birds in the course of the year, while the same garden will have at least ten times as many insects – and those are just the ones that are easy to notice. Imagine a life where you can be thrilled by the first appearance of the year of hundreds of species! Every day would be one to treasure.

That is why we have written this book. Both of us adore all aspects of the natural world, but we are particularly keen to blow the trumpets of the smaller characters in the garden, the overlooked ones – even the reviled ones. Yes, you may dread the coming of the 'bitey, sucky and stingy' invertebrates, and the ones that love to investigate our food shortly after sitting on poo. But in our haste to reject these species, we are denying ourselves the opportunity to observe one of the most fascinating groups of animals on Earth, and marvel at their relatively short yet remarkable lives.

The yearly appearance is just one delightful aspect of invertebrate watching, but there are many others. The world of invertebrates can be brutal, from straightforward carnivory and food theft to the more sinister worlds of cannibalism and even eating each other from the inside. But it is also astonishing, and often poorly known; it is an entire universe just waiting to be discovered and enjoyed. We hope that this journey through the invertebrate year will inspire you to look a little closer at our most diverse and fascinating neighbours.

Dominic Couzens and Gail Ashton,
January 2023

Sydney funnel-web spider

Atrax robustus

AUSTRALIA; BODY LENGTH 25–55 mm (1–2¹¹⁄₆₄ in)

THE AUSTRALIAN SUMMER IS IN FULL swing, and, in small, untidy corners of suburbia, the arachnid army is rising. This is no normal awakening of eight-legged creatures; these are special. The Australians are proud of their neighbourhood spiders, in the same way that they often share that their continent is bursting with the most toxic creatures on Earth.

Years ago, my sister moved to Sydney's North Shore and straight away, sited prominently in her kitchen, was a glossy booklet of potentially dangerous invertebrate cohabitees. She had brought young children on her adventure and she felt she needed to know exactly which spiders to fear. Few homegrown Australians buy such booklets, but new immigrants, and especially visiting tourists, are fair game to profit from frissons of arachnid terror.

The truth is, though, that Australia does have some venomous spiders, and some are dangerous, even deadly. The reputation of the continent hinges mainly on one notorious species, the Sydney funnel-web spider. Meetings of early European settlers with funnel-webs didn't always go well (for either party), so a legend was born. Who would believe it – a spider that could kill you? Over the years, about 13 people are known to have met this fate; one unfortunate child died within 15 minutes. Nowadays, antivenoms are widely available, but a bite is still a very serious medical emergency.

This is one of the very few spiders in the world in which the male actually invites the female to eat him during mating. Does it hurt, does the triumph of reproduction surpass everything? It would be interesting to know.

The funnel-web makes a good villain. Even those who despise arachnids can admit that some spiders are elegant, or even beautiful. But the Sydney funnel-web is sturdy, 25–35 mm (1–1⅓ in) in length, metallic black and possessed of outsized fangs that look like weapons. Even as a dedicated lover of invertebrates, it's hard not to recoil at the sight of it. When threatened, spiders rear up and show their fangs, and if they bite they don't let go.

For most of the year, funnel-webs reside in cracks and fissures, or on the ground, and are not met with except during gardening, or endeavours such as clearing outhouses or sheds. However, about now, male funnel-webs, the ones with the deadly bite, are wandering around in search of mates and crossing our paths. Some invariably fall into the pools of affluent Sydneysiders, where they don't drown, but instead curl up and become torpid. Fortunately, they take a while to wake up if met with during a swim.

In many of the very same gardens and yards of suburban Australia lives another dangerous spider – the redback. Its poison is possibly just as toxic, but it lacks the feisty attitude of its neighbour and has much smaller fangs. Nonetheless, deaths from redback spiders are also known, in similar numbers to the funnel-web. This spider is very similar in pattern to its famous North American relative, the black widow (see page 76), with a shiny black abdomen and characteristic red marking. Living in a web above ground, it's easy to disturb when performing a neglected household task. Even if you do have a bad day after getting bitten, it's worth remembering that your suffering at the fangs of a female redback will be less decisive than that of the male. This is one of the very few spiders in the world in which the male actually invites the female to eat him during mating. Does it hurt, does the triumph of reproduction surpass everything? It would be interesting to know.

Oddly enough, despite living cheek by jowl with two genuinely dangerous neighbours, Australians themselves tend to be instead spooked by a different spider species altogether. It can defend itself and bite, but the huntsman isn't dangerous, unless you are prone to a heart attack. Instead, it is very large and extraordinarily fast, and seems to be able to run in any direction from a standing start, even if this is a vertical wall. If one is on the other side of the room, you still feel as though it could reach you in an instant if you lower your guard.

Having heard so much about Australia's dangerous spiders, my first encounter with a funnel-web was not as exciting as I'd hoped. It was in the car park for The Three Sisters, a beauty spot in the Blue Mountains, and it had been unceremoniously squashed. It looked as though it had endured the ultimate ignominy – killed by a tourist.

Common brimstone

Gonepteryx rhamni

EUROPE AND ASIA; WINGSPAN 60–74 mm (2⅓–3 in)

THERE ARE ALWAYS SOME JANUARY DAYS that play tricks, and sometimes the joker is a butterfly. A few years ago, I saw a brimstone in my garden in southern England on 11 January, an unseasonal sulphur sylph lighting up the winter sludge-scape. It did what bright, breezy brimstones always seem to do, appear from nowhere and then dash off to somewhere, as if late for an appointment. But it was, in fact, early – by a good two months – as in the UK the brimstone usually appears in March.

In common with many of our 'spring' butterflies, the brimstone overwinters as an adult. So, in fact, despite early year appearances, the more typical fliers among the daffodils and celandines in February and March are neither fresh nor new; by butterfly standards (many species only live in the adult stage for a fortnight or so), they are very old. All will have emerged from their pupae back in July or August and spent the autumn stocking up on nectar, putting on fat reserves for their winter sleep.

In the diminishing days of autumn, adult brimstones each seek out a sheltered bush or climber and settle down among the vegetation. Their wonderful, scalloped wing-edges so closely resemble leaves that it is virtually impossible to find them, especially among evergreen holly, bramble or ivy. But there they will reside for several months in a state of quiescence as the temperature drops. One of their extraordinary tricks is to synthesize glycerine, which acts as an antifreeze for their body fluids. Another is to expel as much water from their body as they can, to prevent the chances of ice forming in their tissues, which is fatal. Doing this, they can survive in external temperatures below −10 °C (14 °F). They can tolerate being covered in frost and snow.

It is quite a thought that, even in the depths of winter, in a wood or suburb of Europe, you can take a walk and pass by dozens of sleeping butterflies without knowing it.

Many people worry when they see an active butterfly in mid-winter, either a brimstone outside, or perhaps a peacock or small tortoiseshell flapping at a tinsel-decorated window. But this isn't a disaster. An unseasonably warm day will sometimes usher the odd individual from its 'slumber', and a turning up of indoor radiators does the same. But torpor is not an open-and-shut biological state. Aroused brimstones fly around for a few hours and then return to their slumbers, none the worse for the experience – and perhaps, having found a winter flowering plant, dropping off again with a fuller stomach. If you find an indoor butterfly, put it gently in a cardboard box and take it to a shed, loft or outbuilding, and release it on a warm spring day.

The emerging adult brimstones of February and March might be aged citizens, but they are full of vim. Throughout their late summer and autumn lives as youthful butterflies they entirely eschewed reproductive behaviour. But now they feed on early nectar and quickly become frisky, mating and laying eggs in April and May. Having grown old disgracefully, a few adults might even survive to see in the next generation in midsummer. They will look worn and tatty, but they are among the longest-lived adult butterflies in the world. It is a delicious irony that the brimstone is so strongly associated with spring, by its nature ephemeral and brief.

It is quite a thought that, even in the depths of winter, in a wood or suburb of Europe, you can take a walk and pass by dozens of sleeping butterflies without knowing it.

Such is the buttery colour of the male brimstone that there is a school of thought that the name 'butterfly' itself derives from this species and was then expanded to include all of its ilk. It's one of those assertions that is satisfying, but lacks any shred of evidence. Or, to put it another way, it's rubbish.

The truth is opaque and, in a way, far more interesting. It turns out that the word itself is so ancient that its origin is lost in the mists of time. It may derive from ancient times, unrecorded, an era we can only imagine. Maybe, back in prehistory, a hunter's heart soared one day when he or she spotted an early brimstone flitting past the hulk of a grazing mammoth?

Common banded hoverfly

Syrphus ribesii

EUROPE, ASIA AND NORTH AMERICA; WING LENGTH 7–11 mm (¼–½ in)

IN A FEW SHORT WEEKS FROM NOW, INSECT activity will start to hum. And no insect hums quite like the common banded hoverfly, also called the humming syrphus. In high summer, the sounds of many thousands of these hoverflies fluttering their wings will reverberate audibly from the sunlit, deciduous woodland canopy, creating that warm-weather buzz.

At the moment, however, in temperate regions of Europe, Asia and North America, those wings are silent and still. In fact, they haven't formed yet. The common banded hoverfly is still a larva. Strictly speaking, it is a third-instar larva.

Last autumn already feels a long way away, but even in November, there would still have been some common banded hoverflies flying around – the last generation of the year. The females will have then laid their eggs and subsequent first- and second-instar larvae would have fed hungrily on the final available aphids of the year. They would have needed to be suitably merciless to fatten up enough for the long months ahead. Remarkably, these intermediate larvae bedded down with full tummies but without having done the usually necessary pre-diapause poo. Instead, the maggot-like creatures use the black fluids resulting from digestion to accumulate in their hindgut and this helps to help add an extra level of cryptic patterning to the exterior of the third instar, which usually lies prone among the leaf-litter.

There are countless millions of little fireworks everywhere out there, in every dusty drawer of every ecosystem, waiting for spring to light their fuse.

In a way, now, they are at the mercy of the elements. They have shut their development down (this is what diapause is), and are essentially, non-responsive. They have joined the great mass of inert invertebrates that abound everywhere, some as eggs, some as larvae and some as pupae. There are countless millions of little fireworks everywhere out there, in every dusty drawer of every ecosystem, waiting for spring to light their fuses.

There is an arch-enemy to combat first, though, and that is the cold or, to be more specific, the freezing cold. For most living things, ice getting into your body fluids is fatal. It messes up your cells and often causes them to rupture. You are unlikely to survive much of this.

So, diapausing invertebrates that are likely to be exposed to sub-zero temperatures during the winter have two options: freeze avoidance or freeze tolerance. The first option, freeze avoidance, is the option almost everything takes, whatever life-cycle stage it is at. Such animals spirit themselves away in sheltered places, especially underground, where freezing is less likely; cracks in bark, thick leaves and other such spaces are also well populated. And they synthesize chemicals, especially proteins, which act as anti-freezing agents, reducing the temperature at which the body fluids are prone to solidify. Most survive this way.

Smaller is the number that are freeze-tolerant, but the common banded hoverfly is among them. The trick, along with having anti-freezing agents in their cells, is to allow a certain amount of freezing, but in safe places, such as between the cells. If it is so cold that ice forms spontaneously, that is a problem. But instead, the larvae create or ingest ice nucleators, often proteins, which form the 'nucleus' around which ice crystals can form, in appropriate parts of the body. It seems that common banded hoverflies probably get their nucleators from the damp, woodland leaf litter. If it's too dry, they cannot survive.

Of course, insects being insects, it is still more complicated than that. In many parts of this hoverfly's range, the climate is temperate, and any periods of freezing are usually alternated with a thaw. In these uncertain conditions, some larvae may switch from tolerance to avoidance. Perhaps some individual larvae are predisposed to one or the other, affecting their chances of survival.

Whatever system they adopt, common banded hoverfly larvae are astonishingly good at winter survival. They have been known to stay alive in outside temperatures of −35 °C (−31 °F). For an insect associated with hot sunny days, that is pretty astonishing.

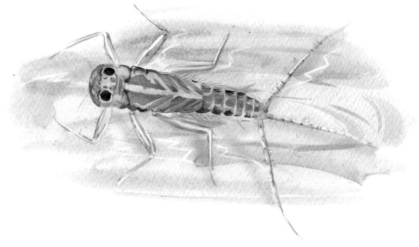

Mayfly

Order Ephemeroptera

WORLDWIDE; NYMPHS TO 50 mm (1 in), ADULTS TO 12 cm (4¾ in)

THE MAYFLY IS FAMOUS FOR ONE THING above all – it 'only lives for a day'. Its apparently sad fate is reflected even in English literature. The Romantic poet Percy Bysshe Shelley, lamenting over the death of his friend John Keats, who died at the early age of 25, wrote in his elegy *Adonais*, published in 1821:

'The sun comes forth, and many reptiles spawn;
He sets, and each ephemeral insect then
Is gather'd into death without a dawn,
And the immortal stars awake again.'

We should admit that the mayfly's single day – and it is often just a few hours – is a good one, though. Mayflies spend their short lives dancing to the tune of reproduction, gathering into mating swarms and doing nothing else but seeking copulation. There is no time to eat during their frenzied hours, but if your time is brief ...

However, on this late winter day, go out into a suitable garden and you can discover something quite different about these apparently cursed insects. Find a pond, dip in your net, scrabble about the aquatic vegetation or the bottom detritus, and see what you can catch. If you find something with a simple body and three filamentous tails, you will uncover the mayfly's secret. It might be a nymph, and it might not be flying around on a warm spring or summer day, but it's still a mayfly, and it's alive! Of course, they don't just live for a day. The nymphs live a quiet, aquatic life, and this can go on for months, even years.

The mayflies' summer raves leave dead bodies scattered all over the water, the riverbank, and waterside vegetation. But they also leave a wide scattering of eggs – mayflies lay among the highest number of eggs of any insect, up to 3,000 per female – and many millions remain intact to launch the next generation. These eggs sometimes lie quiescent over the winter period and hatch in the early spring; others hatch quickly, leaving the larvae, or nymphs, to overwinter. The result is that the mayflies enter into their larval drudgery. They breathe underwater using seven pairs of plate-like gills on the abdomen, which diffuse oxygen from the water. Most species subsist on plant debris and algae. The most exciting thing that they do is to moult as they grow – as many as 25 times. There isn't a lot else to do during the cold, short days. But if there is a message from mayflies, it is that long months spent in the unspectacular art of day-to-day living can lead to a marvellous zenith – the great mayfly dance.

Once spring arrives, mayflies are the only insects in the world to have two separate winged stages; after the last aquatic nymph stage, a somewhat feeble, fluttery-winged, dull-coloured subimago appears and quickly moults into the adult form (there is no pupa). Nobody knows why this extra, non-reproductive stage exists. Its appearance is almost as brief as that of the adult, and in some ways even more perilous. Predators are legion, all keen to make the lives of mayflies shorter still.

Of course, they don't just live for a day. The nymphs live a quiet, aquatic life, and this can go on for months, even years.

There is one delicious irony about the mayfly's ephemeral reputation. Fossils have proved beyond doubt that these insects are among the most primitive in the world. The group first appeared for sure in the Permian period, dating from 298.9 million years ago, and probably arose in the preceding Carboniferous period, from 358.9 million years ago. Mayflies were among the earliest insects in the world to fly and, thus, among the first living things to fly in history. They appeared well before the dinosaurs, and they also survived the world's worst known extinction event, the Permian-Triassic event known as the Great Dying that took place 251 million years ago. About 70 per cent of all known land species died out, including more insects than before or since.

But the mayflies survived, and they do still. And that's a long time for an animal famous for brevity.

Buff-tailed bumblebee

Bombus terrestris

EUROPE; WING LENGTH 13–18 mm (½–¾ in)

 FEBRUARY IN THE TEMPERATE REGIONS OF the northern hemisphere is a tough month. The short days and low atmospheric pressure bring little relief to that cold, damp feeling; these are not ideal conditions for small, cold-blooded animals. Despite the harsh temperatures, the sun is strengthening as the Earth's obliquity slowly tilts the North back towards the sun, and on a clear day, when the wind drops, we can once again feel the heat on our faces from our closest star.

This brief rise in temperature also stirs one of our hardiest insects – the buff-tailed bumblebee – from hibernation. The new queens from last summer's nests have spent the last few months in diapause (where an insect shuts down its development), beneath the ground or in sheltered recesses. These large queens can generally store enough fat, from foraging in autumn, in their bodies to sleep through to spring, but an unseasonably warm day can rouse them from their slumber. If this happens to a queen, she will immediately set about topping up her fuel reserves, so she crawls out of her cosy hibernaculum and into the sunshine.

Bumblebees, like most insects, are cold-blooded. However, due to their size, buff-tailed queens can fly in temperatures that would cause most other flying insects to perish. Their flight is powered by large muscles that attach the wings to the thorax. In the same way that a car engine needs to be warm to function properly, the thorax, which houses the wing muscles, needs to be a certain temperature – around 30 °C (86 °F) – for the muscles to function effectively. To achieve this, the bumblebee pulsates her wings vigorously which, like a tiny kettle, heats up the haemolymph (the arthropod equivalent of blood) in her thorax. Most insects can only become flight-ready when the ambient temperature exceeds around 15 °C (59 °F), but the hardy bumblebee queen, with her larger body and thick fur coat, can get herself prepared in temperatures as low as 5 °C (41 °F). The second she is primed, she takes off and navigates her way to a patch of nectar-rich flowers; the closer the better in order to conserve valuable energy.

Behold the sight of a flying mouse lumbering towards you, trying gamely to keep her considerable mass in the air on those impossibly small wings.

As you stand, face to the sun on that first warm, bright day of the year, you might think you hear the increasing Doppler effect sound of a distant helicopter, then be forced to duck as you open your eyes to behold the sight of a flying mouse lumbering towards you, trying gamely to keep her considerable mass in the air on those impossibly small wings. Queen buff-tails can measure at least 20 mm (¾ in) and weigh almost 1 g (⅟₂₅ oz), and the bigger you are, the more you need to eat; suitable flowers will be fully exploited for their resources. Once replete, the queen will return to her winter boudoir and hit the snooze button until spring, or possibly the next warm, sunny day.

It has become fashionable to 'rescue' winter bees with sugar water and a sense of empathy, however this may be a little misguided. Bumblebees have been coping with winter foraging for tens of millions of years, and probably don't need the urgent care we feel compelled to dispense. If you spot a bee sitting still on a cold day, don't rush to intervene – instead observe it a while. The bee is probably busy warming its flight muscles. If it hasn't moved in some considerable time, it could be moved into direct sunlight to receive a little solar heating. Before offering it sugar solution, place it on a suitable flowering plant – this should provide it with a vastly superior energy hit.

Such hibernal activity is becoming increasingly common. There is increasing winter-colony activity among some bumblebee species as our winters become milder. The problem is that there just isn't enough nectar and pollen available during the winter months to sustain nesting bumblebees. As climate change causes our average daily winter temperatures to edge up faster than plants can adapt accordingly, we must ensure that our winter-garden bumblebees have a good selection of winter-flowering species to keep them going. A selection of organic, early spring bulbs will also help to plug the gap before the warm weather takes hold and nature casts its flowery net over the landscape.

Springtail

Order Collembola

WORLDWIDE; 0.05–17 mm (UP TO ⅔ in)

SPRINGTAILS ARE AMONG THE MOST ubiquitous animals on the planet. They've been around for over 400 million years and were probably among the first arthropods. Since then, they have filled almost every ecological niche available, but because of their size and secretive existence, we know hardly anything about them at all, and this is a huge shame, because they are *fascinating.*

From an evolutionary perspective, the springtails are an interesting bunch because, although they are hexapods – six-legged – and look very much like wingless insects, they aren't actually classified as such. Insects feed with mouthparts that function on the outside of the head, such as the proboscis on a butterfly, or the rostrum on a shieldbug. Springtails, however, have mouthparts that are embedded in a cavity, into which food is inserted to break it down. It is rather more like what humans recognize as a 'mouth' and sets the springtail apart slightly from insects. This, among other features, places it in its own special taxonomic order called Collembola. If you're wondering why they are called springtails in the first place, it's down to a smart little appendage on the underside of the abdomen called a furcula – a spring-loaded fork which, when engaged, flips the springtail into the air; a handy self-propulsion mechanism for evading predators.

Springtails are generally tiny, measuring from less than a millimetre to 6 mm (up to 1/4 in) in length. They look a little like soft-bodied beetles with short legs. They come in many colours, with stripes or spots and some even have thin, metallic scales that make them shine like tiny rainbows. Their eyes are simple – so simple, in fact, that they look like they've been drawn on with black pen, which only adds to their endearing, cartoon-character-like appearance. Things get even cuter with the globular springtails – rotund little creatures with speckles and large eye patches, which make them look like overfed, inquisitive puppies. The largest group of springtails, *Holacanthella* (an endemic New Zealand genus), can reach up to 17 mm (⅔ in), making it a leviathan among Collembolans; it is covered with blunt spikes tipped with orange that give it a distinctly 'licheny' demeanour. Some are also quite hairy, (strictly, insect hairs are made of chitin, not keratin, and are called setae, but we use 'hair' here for simplicity) but because there is a limit to how small a hair can get, some of the smaller springtails are almost overwhelmed by their own bristliness and essentially look like minuscule walking hairbrushes.

Because they are small, wingless and relatively cryptic in habits, these tiny arthropods are very easy to miss, which is quite surprising, because they are everywhere. Every cubic metre of soil beneath our feet can contain up to 100,000 springtails; meaning that even a modest garden potentially harbours millions of them; that's a lot of embedded mouths to feed. So, what are they eating? The short answer is pretty much everything; springtails are generalist detritivores, which means that they essentially eat everything else's leftovers. They form part of the natural composting system, breaking down tiny particles of dead organic matter into even smaller bits that soil bacteria can break down further into essential micronutrients that are then reabsorbed by plant roots. They also regulate the spread of fungi and the make-up of soil, microbial communities through their feeding habits.

So, what are they eating? The short answer is pretty much everything; springtails are generalist detritivores, which means that they essentially eat everything else's leftovers.

Springtails will also snack on plant roots and mycorrhizal fungi and are viewed as pests by many who believe that anything that eats plants is a Bad Thing. Dig a little deeper, though, and things get rather interesting. Studies have found that the feeding action of springtails on root hairs and fungal hyphae in the rhizosphere can actually have a beneficial effect on a plant, by triggering natural responses that send signals to the roots to defend themselves, actually improving growth and resilience in the plant. So, springtails are in fact helping plants to thrive by stimulating growth, which is officially a Good Thing. And let's face it, if springtails haven't managed to destroy the world's plant life in 400 million years, they're probably not going to start now ...

Driver ant

Dorylus spp.

AFRICA; WORKERS 2–8 mm (¹⁄₁₂–¹⁄₃ in),
REPRODUCTIVE INDIVIDUALS 40–50 mm (1¹⁄₂–2 in)

 THERE ARE FEW INVERTEBRATE SIGHTS, or thoughts, more intimidating than army ants on the prowl. The idea of countless millions of these animals running forwards in a never-ending column, catching and immobilizing anything that moves in their path, overwhelming prey with sheer numbers of workers, each motivated unto death, is, quite frankly, scary. For those of us who live in the temperate world, an encounter with a column of army ants can be dreamed of from afar. But for millions of people, especially those following a subsistence lifestyle in rural parts of the world, the experience can be closer to home – even in the garden.

In Africa, many of the army ants belong to a group known as driver ants, and they are a fact of life in rural homesteads, even running around on the lawns of manicured gardens. They live in enormous underground colonies that include anywhere between 300,000 and several million individuals. They are the scourge of every invertebrate that lives nearby on the ground or in low vegetation, with raiding parties radiating out from the nest to catch everything that moves, and some things that don't – they even dine out on the carrion of vertebrates. The workers and especially the massively jawed soldiers, whose duty it is to protect their kin, bite with extreme ferocity. It is fair to say that, with their numbers and their intent, they are unstoppable.

The workers and especially the massively jawed soldiers, whose duty it is to protect their kin, bite with extreme ferocity. It is fair to say that, with their numbers and their intent, they are unstoppable.

And no individual is quite so unstoppable as the queen. Queen drivers are the largest ants in the world (some reach 60 mm/2⅜ in in length), and they are literally the mothers of each entire colony. Their capacity for production is scarcely believable. They can lay eggs at a rate of three million *every month*. That's more than one a second. A queen will mate up to 20 times in its life (the males are winged and prone to wander) and some queens are known to lay about 250 million eggs in their lifetime (their theoretical capacity is the number of sperm they can store, which is 880 million). They are more factory than living creature.

In contrast to the more famous army ants of the Americas, driver ants remain in their subterranean colonies for long periods of time. However, every so often, having cleansed the local invertebrate population, they sense that food is short and the time has arrived for the colony to relocate. This is when the columns spill out into view *en masse* and may then cause problems to confined livestock, or even enter the homes of people. They aren't dangerous, and they don't move very fast, but it is wise to give them a wide berth! They will soon settle and retreat back underground. The blood of every invertebrate within reach, already cold, would run colder at the prospect.

You might expect the blood-and-thunder existence of driver-ant colonies in your back yard to be something of a snag for humanity. But it isn't always so. The Mofu people of Cameroon call the driver ant the 'prince of insects'. When bothered by termites, which ravage their crops and undermine the structures of their mud and straw homes, they know what to do. They seek out the underground colonies of driver ants and bring them in a modified bottle to the entrance to the termite colony. Invertebrate warfare ensues, with only one winner – or maybe two, the driver ants and the grateful Mofu.

And there is another, truly extraordinary way in which the lives of rural humanity and driver ants intertwine. Apparently, countless centuries ago, somebody watched closely and noticed, perhaps in their own pain, how fiercely the driver ant soldiers clamped their outsized jaws on human flesh. Incredibly, one day in the distant past, some unpleasant accident occurred, and somebody had a brainwave. Seeing a stricken colleague, perhaps, with blood streaming from an open wound, they remembered the ants' jaws. With one person holding the wound closed, the other found a soldier ant which, incandescent at the threat to its colony, closed its jaws on the first human flesh it could sense. The ant, its jaws firmly clasping either side of the wound, became a living suture; thence decapitated, it remained in place. The jaws of other soldiers could complete the first aid.

You and I would spot the approach of a driver ant colony with terror. Others, it seems, might think, 'These could be useful.'

Cotton harlequin bug

Tectocoris diophthalmus

AUSTRALASIA; 20 mm (¾in)

YOU CAN FORGIVE SOME TROUBLESOME insects for their sheer loveliness. In the east of Australia, Papua New Guinea and various Pacific islands, the jewel-like cotton harlequin bug is a common sight in gardens and cotton fields. It does some minor damage to cotton and to other plants in the same family (Malvaceae), especially *Hibiscus* shrubs and flowers. It crawls into sunny patches and inserts its mouthparts, which have evolved syringe-like properties, into the young shoots. The sun-drenched snug bug drinks the sap and ought to sigh contentedly, although there is no scientific proof of the latter.

This bug is unusual in a couple of respects, and one of these lies in its extraordinary variation. Every population, regardless of where it occurs, divides into two morphs, one of which is blue, green and iridescent, with multiple variations, and the other of which is orange, also with many different liveries. The two morphs were once thought to be male and female, but both sexes can be either morph. And the distinction is carried through the bugs' short life. Being true bugs (Hemiptera), they eschew the conventional larval and pupal stages, and instead the young, the adult-like nymphs, simply moult frequently and grow in size until they are sexually mature.

The sun-drenched snug bug drinks the sap and ought to sigh contentedly, although there is no scientific proof of the latter.

No one knows why the cotton harlequin bug is polymorphic, but scientists have conducted a great deal of research trying to find out. This has included feeding bugs to birds and mantids (the best known of which is the praying mantis, see page 200) in captivity. The mantids appeared to revel in the experiments, devouring every single bug presented to them. Birds were far more circumspect, and gave them a wide berth, especially after trying them once. Cotton harlequin bugs are closely related to the family known as the stink bugs and exude fluids that are mildly unpleasant. Evidently the colouration, of either morph, is a warning to birds that they are distasteful (aposematic).

However, subtle experiments with the mantids found that being orange could be useful. Mantids see in black and white apparently, and while the iridescent morphs are obvious to them at any distance, the predators can barely distinguish the orange bugs from the leaves around them when they are some distance away. This suggests that orange bugs might have an advantage if lots of mantids are about. But why are any iridescent? The research continues.

The other unusual thing about cotton harlequin bugs is that they are among a very small group of insects to show parental care. In this case, female parents defend their eggs. This is not a case of passionate and devoted service – an experiment showed that, if the females were removed from their eggs for more than a few minutes, they simply forgot about them – life moved on and there was sap to sup. But neither is it time wasted. Another experiment showed that four times as many eggs hatched from guarded clutches than from unguarded ones.

The average cotton harlequin bug lays about 100 eggs in a cluster around a branch or leaf. Its defensive method involves little more than standing on them. If a potential predator comes along – and this is often, somewhat unhelpfully, a hungry nymph of the very same species – the female will flutter its wings and look as ferocious as it can. Clearly there is some deterrent, although the females are apparently defenceless against parasitoids, such as wasps.

This is not a case of passionate and devoted service – an experiment showed that, if the females were removed from their eggs for more than a few minutes, they simply forgot about them

Fortunately, for the female, guarding is a low-risk strategy. No female bug appears to be harmed in any way during the guarding period. They don't suffer greater mortality, or even from weight loss. They often feed during their stints and are not able to recognize their own clutches. They are not sacrificial mothers.

However, it is a great deal more than most insects do. At least they often wrap their young in cotton.

Ashy mining bee

Andrena cineraria

EUROPE; FOREWING 9–11 mm (½ in)

IF YOU START TO BECOME INTERESTED IN bees, one of the first things you learn is how many different sorts there are. Everybody knows about the honey bee (see page 68). It is a species and a brand. Its hives are like giant corporations, famous and dominant, which get most of the bee publicity and the credit for their effect on the world. People also love homespun companies with a charismatic managing director – in other words, the colonies founded and run by a queen bumblebee. But as with so many economies, the true heart and engine of the pollinating economy is made up of thousands of small businesses run by sole traders. These are the solitary bees. In the UK, there are almost ten times as many solitary bee species (220) as there are bumblebee species. And you may be surprised to know that they are among the very best pollinators of all.

Solitary bees are a marvel that you might not have heard of. They are generally small, especially compared to those wide-bodied jets the bumblebees, and they tend to be furtive and retiring. It is very difficult to tell the many species apart. However, it is now, in the spring, that they truly come into their own, and this is particularly true of a group called the mining bees. Many revel in spring flowers. The ashy mining bee, featured here, is one of the few that is easily identified, with its smart, bold, black-and-white stripes. It particularly adores the blossom of fruit trees such as apple, pear and cherry, and is one of their most reliable pollinators.

One of the reasons why solitary bees do a better job of pollinating than honey bees and bumblebees, lies in their terrible table manners. When honey bees visit flowers, they place the pollen in 'baskets' on their hind legs. The basket is a cavity in the tibia surrounded by hairs and, when a honey or bumblebee forages, it soaks the pollen with saliva from its long tongue and adheres it neatly and tidily to the basket, sometimes moistened with nectar, too. However, solitary bees have a much simpler arrangement of long hairs on the legs and/or the abdomen, and the dry pollen stays on these in haphazard fashion, with inevitable high levels of spillage. This messy process is, of course, ideal for transferring pollen between blooms. These bees are the bees' knees.

Each female leaves a small, volcano-shaped pile of excavated soil beside the burrow entrance. These volcanoes and the comings and goings of the bees can be quite obvious and provide terrific entertainment if you stop to watch.

The name 'mining bee' derives from the habit, shared among many solitary bees, of making nests underground by burrowing into the soil; they use their jaws to break up the particles and their legs to sweep out the soil. The burrow might be in bare ground, on footpaths or closely cut lawns, often south-facing. Suitable habitats may be in short supply, and ashy mining bees often dig burrows in very close proximity to each other – the multitudes making them seem far from solitary. However, each female is entirely responsible for her own earthworks, and typically leaves a small, volcano-shaped pile of excavated soil beside the burrow entrance. These volcanoes and the comings and goings of the bees can be quite obvious and provide terrific entertainment if you stop to watch.

Each burrow contains an average of four underground side-branches, and into each one the female places a ball of pollen and nectar, upon which she lays an egg. She seals off each cell and eventually covers the main entrance, too, before making the next. Intriguingly, solitary bees know the sex of their eggs. Males emerge first in the spring, and the cells nearest the entrance invariably house males.

It is an extraordinary effort to construct the burrow and provide for the young, and it is also fraught with danger. Leaving the unfinished burrows open when foraging enables a wide range of parasites to steal in and lay their own eggs. Kleptoparasites such as bee-flies (see page 52) and various species of cuckoo bee are only too keen to exploit the rich larders underground. They lay their own eggs within the burrow or cells, and their larvae steal the food, or worse.

In a colony, with helpers, such parasites could be spotted and evicted. But the sheer number of holes and burrows made by each year's cohort of bees ensures that, at least overall, many are left unmolested, and the sole traders make a profit.

Peacock butterfly

Aglais io

EUROPE AND ASIA; WINGSPAN 50 mm (2 in)

THE PEACOCK BUTTERFLY IS ONE OF THE signature sights of spring from western Europe to eastern Asia. Its bright, vermilion-red wings with large, sapphire eye spots make it among the most distinctive of butterflies.

By early March, the Palearctic days are lengthening and the sun's warmth begins to penetrate winter's frosty armour. The garden is giving us tantalizing glimpses of the summer to come; buds begin to open on trees and the hard, bare ground offers up small, green rosettes of fresh growth. Some of these nascent shoots may be part of your horticultural plan, and some may not, as seeds dispersed in the previous autumn's winds have settled in your soil and are now taking their chances among your herbaceous borders. If you're lucky, these interlopers will be stinging nettles. Yes, I do mean lucky, because the presence of this 'bothersome weed' ensures that this most stunning and beloved butterfly will be able to fulfil its ultimate destiny – to breed.

The peacock butterfly adult is highly cosmopolitan in its nectaring habits, visiting a wide range of flowers in our gardens, parks and field margins. The larvae (caterpillars), however, are much choosier, requiring copious quantities of stinging nettles to munch through on their journey to pupation. The adults overwinter and will seek out crevices in tree bark and walls, and even subterranean nooks such as rabbit holes, where they can survive in temperatures as low as –20 °C (–4 °F). Occasionally they will venture indoors to find somewhere to enter dormancy; you may have a surprise autumnal encounter with one in your house, garage or shed as one appears suddenly, disturbed from its cosy little nook when you draw the curtains, or run a duster down the side of your wardrobe.

Come early spring and they will emerge from their slumber into the sunshine; sassy, semaphore beacons tumbling on the fresh spring breeze. Males are highly territorial, and for good reason; they are in a race to claim the best nettle patches, because it is the best nettle patches that will secure a partner and therefore a continuation of their lineage. At this point in the season the vegetation is little more than ground cover, and the males need to get in early to secure prime real estate, ideally on a gentle slope in full sun. As more males emerge, things can start to get a little heated and fierce battles for territory erupt among the burgeoning foliage, as they joust and spar to claim their territories. The losers must vacate and take their chances elsewhere; the winners get to sit and wait for females to arrive, whereupon the fighting turns to wooing. Unusually for insects, peacock butterflies are monogamous – they will stick with one partner through the mating process. The female chooses the male with the most desirable attributes and – importantly – land, for this is where she will lay her eggs (50–80 on average, but sometimes up to 200) on the undersides of the greenest, freshest nettle leaves. The eggs, small, green and pinstriped like miniature gooseberries, hatch into tiny little caterpillars, which, after eating their own eggshells, immediately set to work on the tender shoots, moulting every week or so until, at around three weeks they are around 40 mm (5½ in) long, velvety black and covered in formidable spines. Siblings tend to stick together, feeding *en masse* in large clusters that will rapidly strip vegetation. If threatened, the cluster will begin 'shivering' in sync with each other to deter predators.

As more males emerge, things can start to get a little heated and fierce battles for territory erupt among the burgeoning foliage, as they joust and spar to claim their territories.

The adults also have highly effective defence strategies. The undersides of the wings are dull, mottled brown, which provides superb camouflage and renders the butterfly virtually invisible in many circumstances. Should a predator, for example, a blue tit, see through the subterfuge and persist with its offensive, the peacock brings out the big guns. It flashes open those bright red wings vigorously, revealing the large eye spots. The purpose of this is to discombobulate its attacker, diverting attention from the soft, vulnerable body. When viewed upside down, the larger eye spots lead down into a point that looks remarkably like the face of a bird, which is known to startle avian aggressors. But that's not all. The peacock can actually emit a warning noise too; the chafing together of the fore- and hindwings produces a broad-frequency hissing sound that is audible to humans. Studies show that this noise repels mice and other small rodents, proving that the peacock butterfly is not just a pretty 'face'.

Dark-edged bee-fly

Bombylius major

EUROPE, ASIA AND NORTH AMERICA; 6–12 mm (¼–½ in)

IF YOU'VE NEVER HEARD OF THE DARK-EDGED bee-fly, let me introduce you to an extraordinary insect. It is a fly, true, but it is more like a cross between a soft toy and a hummingbird. It hovers in front of spring flowers and possesses an extraordinarily long 'nose', the proboscis, half the length of its body, which can probe deep into tubular flowers for nectar and pollen, just as a hummingbird does. And, in contrast to most flies, it is covered in thick, dark, soft hairs. This makes it look like a bee, and the resemblance is intentional; completely unarmed, it nonetheless looks like a more formidable potential foe. It even buzzes like a bee. Overall, anybody who learns about a bee-fly and spots one in the garden or neighbourhood almost invariably becomes a fan. Bee-flies have even been labelled 'cute'. Not bad for a relative of a bluebottle.

Another joy of this insect, found in much of the northern hemisphere, lies in the timing of its appearance. It isn't a harbinger of spring, like an early butterfly or bumblebee, it's the confirmation of spring. It won't fly unless the outside temperature is at least 17 °C (63 °F), and it revels in the sun like a grateful holidaymaker. It often basks on the ground. If it rains, it shelters under dead leaves. It visits our favourite spring flowers, such as grape-hyacinths, primroses, violets and the white blossom of cherries and other early delights, and it doesn't appear until at least March. People meet bee-flies with happy hearts.

However, the dark-edged bee-fly has indeed a dark edge to it. Its adorable countenance conceals a violent past. Once uncovered, you can almost imagine a bee-fly protesting, 'But you need to understand. I was different then. I was still a larva ...'

However, the dark-edged bee-fly has indeed a dark edge to it. Its adorable countenance conceals a violent past.

Bee-flies are members of a vast community of insects that are known as parasitoids – parasites that aren't just annoying or abusive to their hosts, but also kill them. It is simply incredible how many species follow this lifestyle. It is estimated that, around the world, about 40 per cent of *all insect species* are parasites (non-fatal irritants) or parasitoids. They are like family secrets – great in number but rarely talked about.

In the case of the bee-fly, the hosts are solitary bees (see page 44), which abound in gardens, especially in the spring. Many species of host excavate burrows for their young, laying their eggs in side-chambers and leaving a heathy snack of pollen and nectar inside for when each larva hatches. These chambers are well underground, and it is far too risky for a physically defenceless fly to enter the burrow to lay its eggs. So, the bee-fly has evolved a truly astonishing solution.

That solution is akin to carpet bombing. The bee-fly hovers above the entrance to a burrow, or a cluster of solitary bee burrows, and drops its eggs from a height so that they land inside or next to the burrow. To do this, its egg-laying tube, the ovipositor, is fitted with a spine, allowing the insect to 'flick' each egg down and slightly forwards with a twitch of its abdomen. If you are fortunate enough to catch sight of a bee-fly near some of these holes, you might even see these jerks of the body in mid-hover.

Amazingly, prior to laying eggs, the female bee-fly squats near the soil, as if defecating, and dusts the tip of her abdomen. The eggs are then coated in dust individually as she lays them. It is possible that these grains adhere to each egg and add extra ballast, making the aerial bombing more accurate. It is also likely that the dust-coated eggs are camouflaged for protection.

At any rate, once the eggs hatch, each larva – which has several pairs of false legs – crawls deeper into the burrow and towards the brood-chambers. Its first antisocial act is to steal the food resources meant for the bee's larva. It gorges upon these and grows rapidly, at the same time condemning the host's larva to death by starvation. But then, just to make sure, it metamorphoses into a bigger larva with a taste for flesh and eats the host grub. Thus satisfied, it can then pupate and spend the long months underground – until it emerges as the bee-fly we know and love, with a fresh and furry makeover.

Luna moth

Actias luna

NORTH AMERICA; WINGSPAN 80–115 mm (5–4½ in)

WARM NIGHTS IN THE EASTERN USA bring with them the emergence of one the territory's most beguiling creatures. Luna moths (also known as American moon moths) are ghosts of the night – pale ephemera with a purpose, seeking love on the merest hint of a breeze.

This is one of America's largest moths with a wingspan of up to 130 mm (5 in) and, with those long, slender tails streaming behind, it is essentially as broad as it is long. It has adapted for life across a large land mass with varying seasonal fluctuations; in the northern reaches it is univoltine, meaning it produces a single brood in a year, whereas in the warmer Southern states it is bivoltine or even trivoltine, producing multiple generations in a breeding season.

It begins with a clutch of tiny eggs, mottled white and brown, like a spoonful of puy lentils stuck to the leaf of the caterpillar foodplant (the luna is a moth of cosmopolitan tastes – birch, walnut, liquidamber, ash and willow are all very much to its liking). Within 1–2 weeks the eggs hatch into little, green caterpillars covered with fountainous, spiny adornments, which give them a feisty punk look. This will not last for long though, as each caterpillar must eat and eat until it, quite literally, bursts at the seams. It will moult several times throughout its larval stage, each time becoming larger and pudgier as it stockpiles energy and nutrients for the really big change; it is a biomass converter to the extreme.

When the time comes to pupate, the caterpillar changes colour from green to brown, for no longer must it blend in with the leafy canopy and it now has to drop to the ground and remain unseen among the leaf litter. There it spins a silken cocoon around itself, to give it some protection from predators and provide a moisture barrier, which prevents the formation of pathogenic fungi. Within the cocoon it begins to pupate, almost completely changing its external appearance. Once the alchemy is complete, the adult luna moth births itself out of the cocoon as a very different beast. It is now furry, long-legged and sporting a large and valuable set of antennae, the importance of which will be revealed shortly. But where are its magnificent green wings? All that can be seen at this stage are crumpled-up balls on its back – they look more like they've been left at the bottom of the laundry bag, but the moth scuttles to a safe nook and begins to redistribute air and haemolymph around the body, pumping it into its wing veins. As the wings slowly inflate, they take that familiar and stunning form of pale chartreuse panels, outlined with magenta and, in the centre, those elegant, mystical-looking circles that look like moons in partial eclipse, from which this moth's common name derives. Two long, elegant tail-streamers extend back ostentatiously. These 'tails' look beautiful, and possibly are a courtship tool, but they also serve a much more practical purpose, because research has found that they can scramble the echolocation signals of bats, which is useful when you are a large, nocturnal moth and essentially a flying meal.

The fully formed, flight-ready adults now need to find each other in the dark, often across long distances. Time is of the essence – adults do not even stop to feed and thus evolution long ago dispensed with functioning mouthparts. To accelerate the dating process further, the female luna moth emits a pheromone from a gland towards the tip of her abdomen. The power of this pheromone cannot be overestimated and could be likened to Marilyn Monroe turning up at a military airbase in 1954. The pheromone carries on the breeze and any males in the area will pick up the scent through their super-sensitive, feathery antennae. They are hit with the full force of an intoxicating sensation that instinct simply will not allow them to ignore. It's then just a matter of who can fly the fastest, and who can avoid the bats on the way ...

Research has found that they can scramble the echolocation signals of bats, which is useful when you are a large, nocturnal moth and essentially a flying meal.

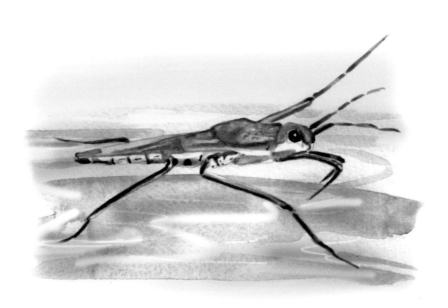

Pondskater

Family Gerridae

WORLDWIDE; 10–15 mm (⅖–⅗ in)

THERE ARE MANY INVERTEBRATES THAT live on land, and plenty that live in water. But living *on* water? This is a fairly exclusive niche, neatly occupied by the pondskater, a widespread and gregarious insect known by various names globally; water skeeters, water striders and water skimmers, to name but a few.

If you are lucky enough to have a largish pond in your garden or local green space, then the chances are that it will be frequented by a pondskater. And where there is one, there are usually *lots*. As the sun warms the surface of the water, these skinny skimmers edge out into the middle of the pond to absorb some solar power. They move cautiously, inching their way out of the shadows beneath overhanging vegetation. They will gather in numbers, hanging out on the water, their feet making teeny concaves in the water's surface tension.

Pondskaters are a fascinating group of animals that bridge the divide between the aquatic and terrestrial insect. The former spends most of its life in the watery depths of freshwater ponds, lakes, rivers and even puddles, either as larvae or throughout its adult phase too. The latter tends to stay away from water, because terrestrial insects and liquid don't mix very well; a difficulty that the pondskater has overcome with the help of a few evolutionary quirks.

Pondskaters are members of the Gerridae, a family of true bugs (Hemiptera) with a slender, lightweight body held aloft on long, stilt-like legs. The body plan may look similar to many other bugs, but the devil is in the detail. Unlike the terrestrial invertebrate body, the pondskater's entire exterior is covered in hydrophobic 'microfuge hairpiles'. These micro-hairs completely repel water, so that the skater cannot collect moisture and become weighed down (imagine how heavy a single droplet of water must be, when you measure and weigh less than half a matchstick). Pondskater legs are very long and radiate out from the body like wheel spokes, creating an extremely broad weight distribution on the surface (think how much more buoyant you are in the water, when you are on your back, with your arms and legs spread out like a starfish). The 'feet' are also highly hydrophobic; tiny hairs trap air, which prevents the pondskater's feet from penetrating the surface. Clever stuff, and critical, because water surface tension is deadly to tiny creatures. Water molecules that come into contact with air bond together, forming the sticky film that we refer to as surface tension. It is practically intangible to us, but on an insect scale it is the equivalent of falling into quicksand; any attempt to free itself will result in the insect becoming more firmly trapped, being sucked into the gloop, and inevitably succumbing to a watery death.

The pondskater's water-repellent chassis not only keeps it buoyant, but also makes it quite the athlete on the surface. The back two pairs of legs move together to propel it at high speed (thought to be the equivalent of around 645 km/h [400 mph] in human terms) on its little bubble pedestals – the locomotion of a rower combined with the velocity of a speed skater. The front legs have claws around halfway down – an adaptation the pondskater shares with the mantids. Because the back four legs are in charge of movement, the front pair are free to scoop, grab and ensnare at will; those pre-apical claws ensuring that prey cannot wriggle free. Pondskaters are ferocious predators. They may look timid and inconsequential, but they are the freshwater equivalent of the top savannah hunters; quick as a cheetah, stealthy as a leopard and as opportunistic as a hyena. They chase down smaller invertebrates with lightning speed, trapping them in bear hugs before spearing them with their needle-like mouthparts, sucking them dry. Any small creatures languishing in the surface tension are easy pickings; even bees, wasps and spiders will become a meal, and many skaters will descend on a victim simultaneously for a piece of the spoils.

Water surface tension is deadly to tiny creatures ... It is practically intangible to us, but on an insect scale it is the equivalent of falling into quicksand

So, while you may think that the pinnacle of apex hunting is the preserve of the Serengeti, take a closer look at your local patch of calm, open water and watch an equally enthralling drama unfold before your eyes – and that is the extraordinary, elegant and deadly water dance of the pondskater.

Backswimmer

Notonecta glauca

EUROPE, ASIA AND NORTHERN AFRICA; 14 mm (⅔ in)

 YOU CAN TRY POND-DIPPING, BUT YOU DON'T even need to dip to find a backswimmer. These feisty hunters spend much of their time motionless on the surface of the water, lying in wait upside-down, and if you disturb them, they will quickly 'row' with their extended, hairy hindlegs down into the depths. They are easy to see now that the warmer weather is here. Having mated in mid-winter, the nymphs have hatched out and are often abundant.

Backswimmers are predators. They have evolved to feed off stricken insects that have accidentally fallen into the water, detecting them initially by their sense of touch. They can be imagined as the equivalent of spiders waiting for the tell-tale pull of silk, the tug of struggle, except that the 'web' is the surface water layer. These animals, with their minute brains, can distinguish prey from other disturbances, such as inanimate objects plopping in to the water, or motions made by other backswimmers. They use the different frequencies of the waves. Once they detect food, each swims rapidly towards the flailing body and sinks its rostrum (modified, sharp, tubular mouthparts) into weak points in the prey's exoskeleton. They are like living, swimming syringes.

The surface is not their only arena, though. Backswimmers are perfectly capable of feeding in mid-water or near the bottom. They are fond of almost anything wriggling, and a particular favourite of theirs is the larvae of mosquitoes. They devour these in such quantities that they have been thought of as potential biological control for the unpopular insects.

Backswimmers are able to despatch truly epic prey, such as small tadpoles and even fish. Human fingers aren't immune to their bad moods, and many a pond dipper has received a painful nip.

Studies even suggest that female mosquitoes avoid ponds with too many backswimmers. Along with these, backswimmers are able to despatch truly epic prey, such as small tadpoles and even fish. Human fingers aren't immune to their bad moods, and many a pond dipper has received a painful nip.

Backswimmers are air breathers and each survives underwater by trapping air bubbles on its ventral surface – this, of course, faces upward when it is upside-down, and makes it much easier to replenish air stocks on its regular forays to the surface, and keeps it buoyant. Recent studies have shown that these humble insects trap air all over tiny hairs on their surfaces, especially on the elytra (the wing-cases) so that they are effectively superhydrophobic. Engineers have found that their trapped air-film is remarkably long-lasting. While most films remain intact for just a few days, that on the dorsal surface of a backswimmer can last 130 days, and even works against a gentle flow. These streamlined insects can cruise effortlessly through the water with minimal drag.

One of the many delights of immersing yourself into the invertebrate wonders of a garden pond is the intrigue one feels about how everything gets there. This is particularly exciting when a pond has recently been dug out. How do the smaller creatures find it? Backswimmers are often among the very first insects to find newly established ponds, and they are likeably indiscriminate about where they settle. They are perfectly at home in fountains, water butts, tanks, unintentionally full buckets and even bird baths. Clearly, they can spread very effectively.

To the surprise of many, they fly. Backswimmers are so completely at home in the water that it's hard to imagine them taking off into the unknown, but that is what they do, especially at night. They have evolved to find water while flying. As soon as they detect polarized ultraviolet radiation from the water below, they have a natural 'plunge reaction'. They stop, align their bodies at an angle, and plop downwards to a new future.

It doesn't always go well. Occasionally they drop onto things that might look similar, such as windows and car windscreens, landing with a thud instead of the intended splash. Presumably then there are red faces all round and the backswimmer becomes a backtracker, regaining the air and its dignity.

It's a rare moment of awkwardness for this astonishing insect.

Western honey bee

Apis mellifera

WORLDWIDE; FOREWING: WORKER 9–10 mm (½ in),
QUEEN 10–11 mm (½ in), MALE 12–15 mm (⅔ in)

THERE CAN BE FEW GARDENS THAT AREN'T visited by honey bees. At the same time, very few honey bees live in a truly 'wild' state. Most of your visitors will come from a hive looked after by a beekeeper, so most are, effectively, domestic animals. It's the equivalent of having cattle grazing on your lawn.

These remarkable insects are appearing in large numbers again after the long winter. Honey bees don't hibernate, but life slows down. There aren't many blooms to find, so almost everyone remains in the hive and survives on the honey they collected over the summer and autumn. Now, though, things are warming up again. The queen begins laying eggs once more, the workers forage and the colony's activity shifts up a gear.

One thing that they might do any time from now is to found a new colony if, for example, the hive is already saturated with honey. The queen expedites this at her initiative, and the process is known as swarming. She simply relocates with a few thousand workers, leaving behind a number of enlarged cells containing the pupae of virgin queens, often about 20 individuals. These potential successors have been fed on royal jelly (a secretion from the heads of workers) for their whole larval lives – drones and workers are fed for only three days with this substance – and should hatch in great condition. But their pampered start in life soon comes up against a brutal denouement. The virgin queens hatch out, become aware of their rivals and immediately all the queens fight to the death. The last one standing takes all, inheriting the old queen's colony.

This new queen takes on responsibility for the workers remaining in the original colony, but worker bees don't live for more than a few months, so she needs to replenish her colony by mating. The queen leaves the hive and makes her way to a congregation point for males (drones) from all the local hives, often in an open area about 10m (33ft) above ground. You might think the bees might look across the dancefloor shyly, but in reality the drones are uninhibited and will do the business quickly in mid-air. Over several days the new young queens will mate repeatedly, and the drones quickly die. During this brief romantic spell, a given queen will acquire all the sperm she needs for the rest of her life to be the reproductive core of the colony. Queen honey bees don't normally live for more than four or five seasons, but they still produce hundreds of thousands of eggs, most of which hatch into the infertile female workers.

The worker bees, for their part, don't spend all their days collecting honey, but instead perform tasks according to age. The younger workers begin with in-hive duties, including keeping the hive cells clean, feeding the larvae and producing royal jelly. After a few weeks, they are promoted to foraging duties or defence of the hive. These are the bees we see out and about, looking busy. If you see a honey bee at your garden flowers, you know it will be at least 20 days old.

One of the most astonishing aspects of honey bee behaviour is their well-known ability to optimize the colony's foraging, by successful workers coming back to the nest and passing on instructions as to where the best and richest nectar sources can be found. The returnees pass on this information by performing a so-called 'waggle dance', which is a coded message. On the comb they follow a rough figure-of-eight pattern. During the straight section between the two circles, the bees waggle their bodies and vibrate their wings. The orientation of this section relative to the horizontal or vertical on the comb structure indicates the direction workers need to follow relative to the sun. The length of the waggle run indicates the distance to travel, and the overall excitement is an indicator of the richness of the source concerned. It is an incredibly sophisticated method of messaging. It's been jokingly suggested that it is a good thing that all worker bees are females, since they are clearly happy to ask directions!

The virgin queens hatch out, become aware of their rivals and immediately all the queens fight to the death. The last one standing takes all, inheriting the old queen's colony.

There is still much to learn about these astonishing insects. Who knows, maybe the waggle dance passes on more information than we realize? Perhaps the bees tell each other how messy our garden is, whether or not the lawn needs mowing and whether we are behind with our weeding? Such information is, let's be honest, much more important to them than it is to us.

Milkweed leaf beetle

Labidomera clivicollis

NORTH AMERICA; 12–13 mm (½ in)

WHILE WE EAGERLY AWAIT THE ARRIVAL of the monarch butterflies (see page 160) to patches of milkweed across the USA and Canada, there is another insect associated with the plant that you may not have heard of: the milkweed leaf beetle. You have possibly mistaken it for a ladybird (see page 80); it is indeed very similar, although it is not part of the Coccinellidae family of ladybirds, but instead one of the Chrysomelidae – a huge family of leaf beetles that are often rotund, brightly coloured and patterned, sometimes even iridescent.

This Nearctic beetle can be found throughout the Midwest and eastern seaboard of North America, wherever milkweed grows. Its head, pronotum and legs are glossy black, with wing casings that can vary from pale orange to deep red, decorated in black spots and splodges, with thin, longitudinal rows of tiny punctures. And these aren't exactly blending in; the colours are typical aposematicism – the adaptation of being brightly coloured to appear distasteful or toxic, although in this case it is a warning to be heeded because this beetle is not bluffing.

As its name suggests, the milkweed leaf beetle feeds on milkweeds, which are highly toxic to the majority of other species. This is handy in itself, because being able to eat toxic plants significantly reduces competition for a food source; your pantry is less likely to be raided by less specialized species. In the case of milkweed, there are several other insects that feed upon it, including the red milkweed beetle (a beetle from a different family – the longhorns), the large milkweed bug and the small milkweed bug, all of which are red and black and are not at all pleasant to eat (a wonderful example of Müllerian mimicry, see page 207). How, though, does this beetle survive eating a plant that can cause serious illness, or even death, in many other animals? It has evolved over millennia to metabolize the cardiac glycosides within the sap of the plant

How, though, does this beetle survive eating a plant that can cause serious illness, or even death, in many other animals?

safely, but that's not all: the chemical compounds bioaccumulate within the beetle's body, rendering it toxic too. Any bird, mammal or lizard foolhardy enough to ignore the visual warning signals and snack on the milkweed leaf beetle will be rewarded with a nasty bout of food poisoning, or worse. Of course, nature has a sense of humour and there are some predators that have also evolved immunity to the toxins, so the milkweed leaf beetle is by no means invincible.

Unlike the monarch butterfly, the milkweed leaf beetle will complete its life cycle upon milkweed plants within a much smaller range. In regions with consistently warm temperatures, there can be several generations in a year, whereas more northerly climes result in one or two successive broods. Eggs are laid on the undersides of leaves and, when hatched, the larvae will feed gregariously for a short while before dispersing prior to pupation. The larvae are wonderfully endearing; pudgy, glossy orange jellybeans that rumble around slowly, eating as they go. They do have a rather macabre side though – as they are known to indulge in a spot of casual cannibalism. The larvae of earlier broods in the season are known to eat some of their later-emerging 'siblings', in addition to the milkweed food plant.

While this may seem counter-productive, it is worth noting that it could be a rather useful strategy for ensuring that the older larvae have a contingency supply of food. Studies have also found that adult females will lay clusters of infertile eggs among viable broods. The infertile eggs are ready-made buffets for the hatchlings, and it is thought that this is a deliberate act by the female to give her young a head start in life. This is important in itself, as the more the larvae eat, the bigger they will be when they emerge from pupation. Larger adults can cope better with food shortages, and lay more eggs, which in turn produce heftier larvae with improved survival rates. Just goes to show how important it is to keep the snack cupboard stocked for the kids.

Black widow

Latrodectus spp.

NORTH AMERICA; FEMALE *c*.15 mm (⅔ in), MALE UP TO 7 mm (¼ in)

BLACK WIDOW – EVEN THE NAME IS ENOUGH to cause a frisson. Nobody messes with this small but potentially dangerous spider, found all over North America as a trio of closely related species. These days it is a symbol of feminine power. Everybody knows that, in spider society, the females are much larger than the males, are choosy, and kill and eat potential mates without hesitation.

The black widow is a common spider, and is found in urban and suburban areas, but it avoids people. It is most often encountered in quiet corners of houses, or in garages and in yards. It spends almost all its time in its web and isn't at all aggressive to people. Bites invariably occur when human and spider come together by accident, perhaps when somebody is cleaning out a shed or room.

Nevertheless, the black widow is potentially dangerous and, indeed, in some Native-American traditions, the spider is a symbol of death. Fatalities have unfortunately occurred in the past, although they have always been very rare. The bite is extremely painful, but symptoms don't usually last for more than a couple of days. Sweating is a common reaction, and sometimes nausea. The venom is a neurotoxin, and its effect on the cells is alarming; it creates pores in cell walls, so that ions flood in and the cell becomes permanently excited. On occasion, this can lead to cardiac arrhythmia and convulsions. It is most dangerous for children and the elderly.

The web is notable for being something of a mess, just a mesh of threads, usually, but not always horizontal. It lacks any of the design expertise of many spiders, but is extremely effective. Widow spiders have a reputation for being able to deal with prey that is much larger and more vigorous than they are, including grasshoppers and cockroaches. The extra-strong venom undoubtedly contributes to this ability.

When it comes to reproduction, the web is somewhat tangled. However, the reputation of the black widow, as well as its name, overstates the degree to which females kill and eat their potential mates. Males often survive and will sometimes run the gauntlet of mating with more than one female. Most are very careful when approaching their love interest, but assertive individuals sometimes damage the female's web by cutting her 'escape' routes, ensuring that they cannot possibly be ignored!

Remarkably, in the western species *Latrodectus hesperus* at least, both males and females produce scents on the silk of their webs. Not only does this ensure that an approaching male will home in on a female of the correct species, it is also possible that females, scenting the air, will have an idea of how many males are around. If population density is high, a female can afford to be choosy.

The male's attempts to mate begin, perhaps surprisingly, on his own web. Spiders don't copulate directly, but instead males spin a specialized mini-web and deposit their own semen upon it. They then insert their palps (sensory appendages near the mouth) until they are filled with sperm, and then go in search of a female. When they copulate, they do so by inserting their palps, one after the other, into a fold in the female's exoskeleton called the epigyne. The epigyne is, if you like, the reception area for the sperm, and it can be stored here before being transferred to the uterus. It is a remarkably indirect method of copulation, but extremely intimate in its way.

The reputation of the black widow, as well as its name, overstates the degree to which females kill and eat their potential mates. Males often survive.

Eggs are laid in batches of 250–700, surrounded by a web, and the female is aggressive in protecting them. It would take a brave predator to attack the brood of this formidable mother.

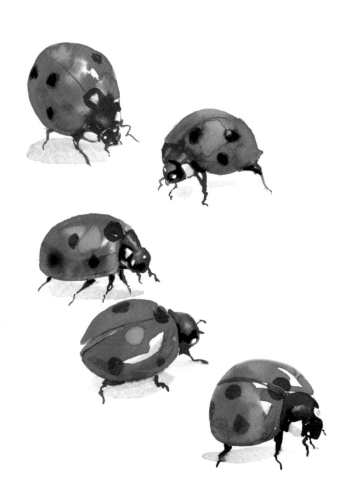

Seven-spot ladybird

Coccinella septempunctata

EUROPE AND NORTH AMERICA; 6–8 mm (⅓ in)

IT DOESN'T MATTER WHAT TIME OF YEAR IT is; whether high summer or the depths of winter, you can always be greeted by the cheery, scarlet hemisphere that is the seven-spot ladybird, and all the better our day is for this encounter. The seven-spot ladybird is the quintessential insect, almost ubiquitous in our lives and certainly one of our favourites. A survey of public opinion by the Royal Society of Biology in 2015 revealed that it was voted the second most popular insect in the UK, bettered only by the buff-tailed bumblebee (see page 28).

We have a long and significant relationship with this beetle; the name 'ladybird' supposedly originates from cultivators of old who, dismayed by the damage caused to their crops by aphids, prayed to the Virgin Mary – also known as Our Lady – for a solution. The arrival –

although probably coincidental – of the hitherto unnamed beetles that set to work eating up the aphids seemed nothing short of miraculous and compelled the farmers to name them Beetle of Our Lady. This progressively compressed into 'lady beetle' and later 'ladybird' or 'ladybug', depending on your geographical position. In Germany it is known as *Marienkäfer*, which translates as 'beetle of Mary', and still today it is seen as a portent of good fortune and happiness throughout its extensive global range. The eponymous seven black spots are thought to symbolize the seven joys and seven sorrows of Mary, and it is considered unlucky to harm or kill this beetle.

The seven-spot ladybird's success as a species is largely down to its ability to adapt to all manner of habitats and climes. It is a generalist, unfussy in its breeding criteria and with a broad diet; and because these ladybirds overwinter as adults, they can capitalize on early warm days to begin mating as soon as possible in the year. In mid-spring, the adults begin to emerge from their winter nooks and crannies; males seek out the larger females and the mating race begins in earnest. Coupling is a protracted process, with the protagonists remaining locked together for some considerable time – anything up to a couple of hours. By hanging onto the female for this long, the male can ensure no rivals will copulate with his partner, and therefore increase the probability that he will perpetuate his lineage.

Successful males will not, however, see the fruits of their labours, for once the female decides mating is over, she will shake off the male and embark on the next phase of her life alone. She finds a suitable site for her young, which will often be within close range of an aphid population. She lays a cluster of tiny, yellow eggs on the underside of a leaf – these slim and ovoid eggs stand to attention, perpendicular to their surface – and here ends her parental duty, for she will leave the clutch and seek another egg-laying location. She does not need to mate again, as the sperm from her original donor is stored internally and dispensed as needed; a reproductive vending-machine, if you like. She oviposits as many times as she can, laying as many as a thousand eggs in her remaining days.

Around a week later the eggs hatch and what emerges from each egg is a tiny, knobbly, black larva with symmetrical red markings – a negative image of its adult self; it is a lanceolate alien with six legs and the blood-thirst of a newborn vampire. For the next few weeks, the local aphid population begins to mysteriously disappear, despatched swiftly by the hungry and highly efficient larvae. It is a perfectly timed interaction; as summer peaks, so do aphid numbers and thus several generations of ladybirds will feast over the warmest months. Once a seven-spot larva is ready to metamorphose, it attaches itself to a stable surface and moults into a globular, hard-shelled pupa, within which it biologically rearranges itself over the next few weeks.

The eggs hatch and what emerges from each egg is a tiny, knobbly, black larva with symmetrical red markings ... a lanceolate alien with six legs and the blood-thirst of a newborn vampire.

What emerges is a pale, spotless (literally) adult which then spends time hardening its elytra; the carnelian red and black spots develop gradually over a few hours. The new adults will spend the remainder of the summer fuelling up in preparation for hibernation. Even during their winter diapause we can find them, tucked in the cracks of tree bark, nestled into dried flower heads and perhaps under our sofas. And if you do see one, the chances are that it will indeed brighten up your day.

German wasp

Vespula germanica

WORLDWIDE; 12–20 mm (½–¾ in)

 LET'S PLAY A GAME. THINK OF YOUR favourite 'bug' and I'll try to guess what it is. Butterfly, bumblebee, ladybird will all be up there with your answers. I also know that what you probably *won't* say is 'wasp'. In fact, it's at the bottom of most people's list of loved animals, and right up at the top of the most hated list. It is therefore my job, in the next few hundred words or so, to change your mind.

Let's start with my use of the very broad term, 'wasp'. Of the 100,000 species (and counting) of wasp currently described, only a few thousand are classified as 'social', meaning that they live in colonies that have an egg-laying queen and workers who feed and tend the eggs and larvae; these are the ones that are most familiar to us while the other 95 per cent or so are solitary species that don't generally interact with humans, and do not sting us.

The wasps we know and (mostly don't) love are the larger, yellow and black warriors – known as 'yellowjackets' – that seem hell-bent on ruining our late-summer picnics and afternoons in the beer garden. They also pack a punch from their rear end, and – because they are social – they will mount a coordinated assault that can leave us in various states of physical distress ranging from grumpy and lumpy to hospitalized. I'm really selling not them to you, am I? Bear with me.

There are just a few social wasps that you may encounter in your garden, and one of them is the German wasp. It is, admittedly, more likely than others to sting you, and although you are probably exasperated by these seemingly unprovoked attacks, what if I were to tell you that we are not so different from this wasp – in fact, we are surprisingly similar?

We first see German wasps in mid-spring, in the form of the surprisingly large queens who thrum past us on urgent pursuit of nectar sources and hunting grounds. The queens have a tough start, as they have each been alone since a brief reproductive encounter with a male the previous autumn. Having overwintered in solitude, this single mother sets about finding a suitable nest site. A dry, sheltered location with enough space for rapid expansion is prime real estate for the German wasp queen. In the natural environment this can be underground, a hollowed-out tree or rock crevice; however, some social wasps take a more synanthropic approach; loft spaces, wall cavities and garden sheds – basically the least frequented areas of our human habitation – are all ideal starter-home sites for social wasps.

For the first few weeks the lone queen has her tarsi ('hands/feet') full; she is the builder, egg-layer, hunter, nanny and security guard until the first worker larvae pupate. From then on, the new workers take over with nursery and hunting duties, although it has been discovered that German wasp social order is a decidedly more relaxed set-up than, say, the ants or honey bees. Rather than having specialists within the nest who stick rigidly to their own roles, German wasp nests have a looser framework of labour in which workers are more free-flowing between roles, yet still keep things ticking over nicely. One task that they do perform in perfect synchronicity, however, is defence, a fact verified by anyone with the misfortune – or foolhardiness – to disturb a colony at peak nesting time. Globally, social wasp colonies face threats from a wide variety of predators, such as badgers, black bears, weasels, raccoons, honey buzzards, honey badgers, mice, rats and even lizards. The coordinated response they mount is an evolved strategy; the instinctive behaviour of a group of females who will do anything to protect themselves and their young in the face of imminent threat – something for which we can all feel some degree of empathy.

We've talked a little about how German wasps look after themselves, but what about the services they provide to the wider world (which inevitably includes us humans)? It is estimated that the average colony will consume at least a whopping 4.3 kg (9½ lb) of invertebrate biomass. That's almost 100,000 flies, spiders, moths and caterpillars. Add to this the many species of aphid and scale insect which, when unchecked, can cause significant damage to food crops and you can see that the yellowjacket wasps are among our most important natural controllers of smaller invertebrates.

The truth is that social wasps are devoted carers who dedicate themselves to keeping their young warm, dry, clean and fed. They are fiercely protective and prepared to go extraordinary lengths to keep their family safe. Sound familiar? Maybe we can keep that in mind and give the social wasps the space they need to feel safe – that way, they will respect us too.

Cuckoo wasp

___

Chrysis spp.

WORLDWIDE; 5 mm (¼ in)

SO, YOU'RE WALKING ALONG A SUNNY, OPEN path on a warm summer's day and something catches your eye. The smallest of glints in your peripheral vision, it's gone as quickly as it appeared, but then you see another, on the ground at the path's edge. You get down on your hands and knees, straining your eyes to focus, to inspect the tiny glimmer and you come face to face with a gemstone of metallic turquoise and red, approximately 5 mm (¼ in) long. But within a flash it's gone, because these things don't stay still for long.

What you have just seen is a jewel wasp, one of the Chrysididae family of wasps. An extremely successful group of solitary wasps, they number around 3,000 described species in 83 genera and are present on every part of the planet except Antarctica. The family is known by several common names, all of which are suitably descriptive; the first, 'cuckoo wasp', pertains to their habit of entering a host's nest – usually other species of solitary wasp – and then laying their eggs next to the occupant's own eggs. Speed is of the essence – the cuckoo wasp must get in, deposit its precious cargo and get out before the host returns; we tend to see them scooting around on the ground, or in dead wood, as they scout potential nest sites. A week or so later, the cuckoo-wasp larvae hatch, then sustain themselves by feeding on the host eggs or larvae, along with any food provisions within the nest cell. Each cuckoo wasp genus is fairly host-specific; for example, *Chrysis* spp. are brood parasites of mason wasps, whereas *Hedychrum* spp. seek out digger wasps. It has recently been discovered that a cuckoo wasp may mimic the scent of its host to evade detection in the nest and increase its own chances of reproductive success.

Another name it is known by is 'jewel wasp', for more obvious reasons; theis wasp has evolved a cuticle surface that shines like polished metal. It can be turquoise, reddish pink or, as in the case of *Chrysis* spp., a combination of both (these get the lovely name 'ruby-tailed wasp'), and the result is tiny, ephemeral gemstones flitting around in the sunshine. The reason for this metallic appearance is due to the structure of the exoskeleton, which is formed of microscopically thin layers of a composite of proteins, lipids, water and a remarkable substance called chitin. Chitin is a hugely abundant (second only to cellulose), naturally occurring polysaccharide, best known as the material that makes up the cell walls of fungi. It also occurs in the shells of crustacea – such as crabs and lobsters – and is the major constituent in insect exoskeletons; a bit of extra hydrogen bonding giving it the strong properties that protect these soft-bodied creatures.

In cuckoo wasps, six chitin-based cuticle layers are arranged in a lattice pattern. Each of the layers of this nanostructure has a space between them that refracts visible light in a slightly different way, producing the glorious iridescence that we see as green, blue and red. If the wasp's instant disco-ball appearance were not sufficiently impressive, then on a microscopic level they are in another league. Cuckoo-wasp exoskeletons have a densely pitted surface, like hammered copper, which intensifies the light-scattering effect even further.

But why, if your *raison d'être* is to sneak into the nest of larger wasps at huge personal risk, would you want the insect equivalent of a hi-vis jacket? While the definitive answer to this question is still something of a scientific quandary, the pitted surface is said to help deflect stings from defensive host wasps, and the iridescence may aid this too. Iridescence is also known to be a cryptic camouflage – the sudden scattering of light off the surface can confuse predators and assist escape. There is also discussion as to whether it helps with thermal buffering against ground heat.

But why, if your raison d'être is to sneak into the nest of larger wasps at huge personal risk, would you want the insect equivalent of a hi-vis jacket?

Besides its more enigmatic methods, the cuckoo wasp also possesses an ingenious and more visible defence mechanism; when triggered, it can fold itself in half. Thanks to a tiny waist (petiole) and concave abdominal underside, it can roll into a tight ball, tucking its head and tail in, leaving the toughest part of that pitted armour exposed to the pointy end of attackers. It's one more trick in the cuckoo wasp's impressive repertoire and goes to show that this wasp has brains, as well as good looks.

Violet carpenter bee

Xylocopa violacea

EUROPE; BODY LENGTH 20–28 mm (¾–1 in), FOREWING 20–22 mm (⅚ in)

EVERYTHING ABOUT THE VIOLET CARPENTER bee is big. It's about twice the size of most bumblebees; it has a big buzz and a big presence. Its body is shiny black, and it is the violet-stained wings that give it its name. It is a stretch limo sort of bee, something special and unusual, the sort that catches your attention. If you are afraid of bees, this one will scare you more. It can theoretically sting humans but, in common with other bees, it has a hundred more important things to do.

For those who live in northern Europe, including the UK, the violet carpenter bee is something of a holiday bonus. It is very common in southern Europe around the Mediterranean, where you often encounter it in coastal resorts, humming around its favourite flowers, often in low blooms in coastal scrub. Wherever it grows, wisteria is a great attraction. In recent years the violet carpenter bee has gradually been expanding north into France and Germany and has even bred and overwintered in Britain. Climate change is allowing it to spread. It is coming; you had better be ready.

Carpenter bees, as their name implies, build their nests in wood. The female has a broad head and very large, powerful jaws, and that means that, not only can this bee burrow tunnels in dead wood, but also into the trunks of perfectly healthy trees. In southern Europe, the violet carpenter bee often selects canes and bamboo, and occasionally structural timbers are used but this is unusual and does not cause problems for householders. It also has a liking for commercial pallets, and on occasion the overwintering adults have been accidentally imported to countries where they don't normally occur.

The violet carpenter bee is a solitary bee, which means that a single female is responsible for building a nest for her young, and there is no social colony, no swarming and no cooperation. In contrast to most solitary bees, the female of this species only makes a modest number of chambers for the next generation, usually only 7–8. She chews a hole about 11 mm (½ in) in diameter and seals each chamber with a mash of wood fragments 2 mm (¹⁄₁₂ in) thick. Perhaps not surprisingly, there don't seem to be any records of cuckoo bees parasitizing this species. One cannot imagine an intruder's fate if it were discovered by an angry, female giant bee. Violet carpenter bees do have venom, and this sort of provocation would cause them to use it.

They will enjoy many weeks of doing not very much except drinking nectar from the many plants that are flowering in the mild climate.

By the time summer is over, the life cycle has been completed, and adults in the Mediterranean, especially the males, sometimes appear again as early as January. They will enjoy many weeks of doing not very much except drinking nectar from the many plants that are flowering in the mild climate. Violet carpenter bees are excellent pollinators, but they occasionally sully their reputation a little by biting holes at the bottoms of tubular flowers to get a short cut to the nectar, instead of squeezing in where they should.

Once the females emerge, the males have a somewhat unsubtle way of showing their intentions. They simply intercept the females, sometimes in mid-air, or catch them when they are visiting flowers. Males may also intercept couples in mid-air, which must be somewhat annoying for everyone concerned. Although males can be territorial, they often simply fly about at random and try their luck.

Happily, not every individual emerges early, and violet carpenter bees can be seen all spring and summer long, with some still around even in September. That's more than a whole season to intimidate the tourists.

Globe skimmer

Pantala flavescens

WORLDWIDE; UP TO 45 mm (1¾ in), WINGSPAN 70–80 mm (3⅛ in)

RIGHT NOW, GLOBE SKIMMERS WILL BE flying over every continent of the world except Antarctica. They are rare in Europe, but they are found everywhere else, even on Rapa Nui (Easter Island), one of the world's most isolated clumps of rock, 3,500 km (5,600 miles) from the nearest continental land mass. They have also been seen at 6,200 m (20,300 ft) in the Himalayas. By far the most widespread dragonfly in terms of distribution, the globe skimmer is truly a citizen of the world. DNA studies have shown that it is composed of a single genetic population, constantly mixed by individuals travelling far and wide. If you see one in a garden in the USA, it is the same genetically as one in Australia. And that isn't the globe skimmer's only remarkable claim to fame.

It is summer in the northern hemisphere, and dragonfly time. It is always dragonfly time in the tropics. These incredible animals patrol almost every freshwater habitat in the world, but they need the sun on their backs. Once airborne and pumped, though, dragonflies are arguably the most efficient predators of any kind in the entire world; about 95 per cent of every attempt at in-flight capture of smaller flying insects is successful. They have astonishing eyesight, thanks to around 30,000 small eyes in the compound whole, each of which can resolve colour, ultraviolet and polarized light. They are also among the world's most efficient flying insects. Each of the four wings is independently controlled, meaning that they can hover, fly straight and fast, fly upside down and backwards. They each have six strong legs and fearsome mouthparts that slice through every exoskeleton. You can imagine an evolutionary flip giving them a chance at world domination.

And perhaps the ultimate dragonfly is the globe skimmer. It's not the biggest, and certainly not the most colourful, in an order of insects that can be stunning. But it turns out that it has always been harbouring an astonishing secret, one that has only recently been uncovered by humanity.

For a number of years, globe skimmers in parts of Asia have gained a reputation for turning up, seemingly from nowhere, in large numbers. About now, for example, they have appeared with the summer's south-west monsoon in northern India. Later on, they will descend on southern India and Sri Lanka. In Africa, they 'appear' at year's end. For a while, these appearances were not thought to be related. Now, thanks to some clever detective work, we know that they are.

The key was a series of observations made by Dr Charles Anderson, a marine biologist who lives and works in the Maldives. These islands should be a dragonfly black hole, since there is no standing water there, and therefore nowhere for the insects to breed. Nonetheless, every October they appear on this archipelago 1,931km (1,200 miles) off the coast of India, and they swarm in their millions, massing in the skies and perching on vegetation at dusk. The globe skimmers appear for a month or two, and then simply disappear.

Meanwhile, though, a little while later, these dragonflies mysteriously appear in the Seychelles, and later in East Africa. Putting two and two together, the tentative conclusion could be that the Maldivian globe skimmers are setting off to cross the Indian Ocean. But that's a long way, more than 2,000 km (1,200 miles). This is an insect that reaches a maximum of 50 mm (2 in) long and weighs 0.3 g (⅒ oz). Could it be possible?

It's not the biggest, and certainly not the most colourful in an order of insects that can be stunning. But it turns out it has always been harbouring an astonishing secret.

The only way that it is possible would be for the globe skimmers to use the prevailing monsoonal winds. At an altitude of 1,000–2,000 m (3,300–6,500 ft) and above, the trade winds are north-easterly; if the dragonflies reach that high, which they are able to do using thermals, they can use these brisk winds to bring an Indian Ocean crossing within range.

It is now thought that globe skimmers perform an extraordinary loop migration around the Indian Ocean, over four generations. The summer generation breeds in southern India and migrates across to East Africa. It arrives and breeds, using seasonal rains. The next generation moves south, breeds again, and moves north towards the Horn of Africa. It then catches the south-west monsoon, which takes it back across to northern India, where it breeds again in the wet conditions. The whole loop is a journey of 16,000 km (10,000 miles).

It is a globe skimmer indeed.

Rose chafer

Cetonia aurata

EUROPE; 14–21 mm (½–¾ in)

 CAN THERE BE SUCH A THING AS A feel-good insect? If so, nominations are now open. To set things rolling, how about that benign beauty of the European summer garden, the glorious rose chafer?

It's fun seeing bees buzzing around blooms, and butterflies are like flower blooms in perpetual motion. But when it comes to sheer character to go with the bling, the rose chafer is a showstopper. When it lumbers into view, you take notice.

You can see from the illustration that the rose chafer is a brilliantly iridescent, golden-green beetle; it is copper below. It also has curious pale markings on its back, as if somebody had been tasked to give the bronze leaf a polish and had overdone the job, causing chafing. Many beetles have brilliant, reflective surfaces on the elytra, and the colours have intrigued scientists for centuries – indeed, it is thought that the insects have borne these vivid colours for more than 50 million years. They are structural modifications in which interference causes light reflection, rather than pigments in the cuticle. A close look at the rose chafer's cuticle has shown an odd effect on polarized light, which presumably is detected by the insects themselves.

If you have it, flaunt it, and the rose chafer makes very little attempt to be inconspicuous. It feeds on a variety of different parts of the plant, including nectar, pollen and the flowers themselves (including roses, hence the name). When these ungainly beetles feed on tight flower heads with lots of blooms, they appear so completely immersed that, fancifully, they could be taking a foam bath. And you can imagine them singing, too.

The approach of one of these beetles is accompanied by a loud hum, and they are fast and powerful flyers, an insect version of wide-bodied jets. Their flight is quite unusual because, in contrast to most beetles, they can close their shiny forewings, the elytra, while flapping their hindwings. Most beetles swing the two elytra aside when flying, without flapping them. However, the rose chafer has a curved notch along its wingicases, so it can fold the elytra away, so to speak.

The colours have intrigued scientists for centuries – indeed, it is thought that the insects have borne these vivid colours for more than 50 million years.

Rose chafers also have another unusual adaptation, a somewhat technical one related to their mouthparts. The long and the short of it is that they have bristles covered with fluid and these help to mop up pollen.

The summer season is brief, and the females soon lay eggs in the soil and the grubs feed until early autumn, go into diapause and resume feeding in the spring. By early summer they spin a cocoon and, after a year of life, the adults form under the soil. However, they remain in the cocoon over the next autumn and winter before emerging the following year. Sometimes they surprise people by emerging from flowerpots.

In the case of most insects, mating is everything. But you do get the impression with the rose chafer that there's nothing really quite like the next meal, especially with the sun on its back.

Common red soldier beetle

Rhagonycha fulva

EUROPE, INTRODUCED TO NORTH AMERICA;

8–10 mm (⅓–½ in)

IN MUCH OF THE NORTHERN HEMISPHERE right now, the days are long and rich. They are the entomologist's happy hour, a time to get drunk on biodiversity. If you have a garden in the UK, even a comparatively ordinary one, at a conservative estimate there will be 500 species around now that you might reasonably see. There are invertebrates on the ground, in the soil, under rocks, in the cracks of walls, in the pond and in all the vegetation. There are invertebrates in the air; you can literally hear the buzz of heavy airborne traffic. You could spend all day searching and watching and not run out of things to see. And of course, there is a lot going on and much of that can be summed up in a single word – reproduction.

If ever an insect was representative of the wondrous, abundant, hell-for-leather world of the summer invertebrate, it would have to be the common red soldier beetle. It is the loose change of the invertebrate summer. It is very easy to find. Just look for any flower head, and it will be there, on the dancefloor. It lives a brief life in which it eats and has sex. It doesn't travel far, and it has no ambitions other than those mentioned.

Unless you are an entomologist, you don't know yet that, in summer, the flower heads of the plants known as umbellifers, or Apiaceae, form a mecca for insects. But find any carrot, or in Europe a plant such as a hogweed, and you will find a whole community of insects on their flat-topped, raised floral umbrellas, including flies, bugs and beetles gorging themselves on nectar. Each flower head is the perfect stage on which to meet. You might meet your partner, but you might also lock eyes with something that kills you.

Of all the umbel-dwellers, the common red soldier beetle must surely be the most enthusiastic and obvious lothario. It has acquired such a reputation among British entomologists that it is colloquially called the 'hogweed bonking beetle'. Couples wander around the flowers so casually that you can imagine each individual absent-mindedly reading a different newspaper to its partner while still sexually engaged. The couple will even prey on aphids and other insects without the need to disengage. It is of course in the male's interest to stick around on the female's back to deter other males from seeking the female's charms. But their sheer audacity is impressive, and rather charming.

Of course, they might as well enjoy themselves. Predators lie around every corner and their average lifespan, which is the same for both sexes, is a mere four days. The summer flirtation is brief indeed. Individuals don't wander much. In one study, the maximum range, for a male, was 400 m (1,300 ft). There isn't really time to see the world.

Of course, all that copulation produces its fruit, and the females quickly drop to the ground to lay their eggs in secret, away from the prying eyes of gardeners. They oviposit in soil, at the base of summer long grass, and fly away to die.

Their larvae, as is so often the case, vastly outlive their parents. They are maggot-like and spend the entire autumn and winter in the soil. They are highly carnivorous, and take a considerable toll on their neighbours, which in this case includes many slugs and snails.

Of all the umbel-dwellers, the common red soldier beetle must surely be the most enthusiastic and obvious lothario.

They pupate in the spring, and when the long days warm the soil they emerge into the bright sunshine, as adult beetles. They have one task, and probably only one thing on their minds.

Garden tiger moth

Arctia caja

NORTH AMERICA AND EUROPE; WINGSPAN 50–80 mm (2–5⅛ in)

TO HUMAN EYES, THE GARDEN TIGER MOTH is a marvel. Many people are astonished that such a stunning creature could be flying around their gardens at night. They think it should be a butterfly. The sight of this wonderful moth can enhance a person's love for nature; memories are made of such encounters.

To the rest of the natural world, however, the garden tiger is repellent – literally. The gaudy colours are a classic case of warning, so-called 'aposematic' colouration. From its hairy larval stage, often nicknamed 'woolly bear', through to adulthood, the moth stacks its body with a battery of unpleasant toxic compounds, enough to cause serious harm to a predator. Those that mess with the garden tiger get a rude shock to their taste buds and insides; they don't make the same mistake twice, linking the bright colours to unpleasantness. And just in case a curious bird or other animal strays too close, the moth can suddenly open up its wings to reveal scary spots on the hindwing, another message to keep away.

Once night falls, however, no amount of bright colour is going to keep the garden tiger safe. After the sun has set, a great and ancient battle recommences that began about 60 million years ago. It is a battle of wills, wits and, primarily, sound. The conflict, of course, is between bats and moths. It is ultrasound combat. And it's taking place above you, in the night sky.

Bats are serious predators of night-flying insects. They have evolved echolocation to catch them and other prey. Echolocation works like sonar, in that the bats make super-fast ultrasonic clicks, and read the echoes that come back to their ears. The system is so efficient that bats can navigate the night sky with complete confidence, avoiding obstacles and homing in on fast-moving prey. These mammals are extraordinary in their own right.

Those that mess with the garden tiger get a rude shock to their taste buds and insides; they don't make the same mistake twice.

However, moths aren't sitting ducks – or, for that matter, flying ducks. They don't just accept their fate in the jaws of a supreme predator. They fight back, in many different ways.

The most obvious way is to hear the bats coming. Many species of moths, including garden tiger moths, have ears that are tuned to the usual frequencies of the bats. When a bat begins to home in on prey, its echolocation changes so that the pulses are much quicker. This means that a moth can tell when it has been 'spotted', so to speak. This allows it to take evasive action, switching its flight to crazy, unpredictable loops and swerves and often simply dropping on to the ground, where the echolocation doesn't work.

This, of course, doesn't suit the bats. Some species, therefore, have evolved something known as 'stealth echolocation'. This means they switch to either higher (200 kHz or more) or lower frequency (down to 12 kHz) clicks that the moth's ears cannot pick up and so don't hear them coming. Another method, used by European barbastelle bats is to use the same frequencies for echolocation but at a much lower intensity, sometimes as much as 100 times lower. Their approach is so quiet that the moths, even those with ears, cannot hear them.

Another weapon that moths, including the garden tiger, use is to make their own clicks, to interfere with the bats' sonar. Most of these moths have sound-producing organs located at the front of the thorax and give off their own ultrasonic clicks and squeaks, up to 4,000kHz, which must overwhelm the bats' signals. Hawk moths produce a similar sound by rubbing their genitals against their abdomens. These signals at best warn the bat that the moth is unpalatable, but some are known to jam the bats' radar and overload the signal, rendering it useless to the bats.

If you think that's amazing, did you ever wonder why moths are furry and soft to the touch? Recent studies show that the hairs also act to dampen the bats' echolocation and absorb the sound, rather than reflect it. And the wings, with their multiple scales, have also evolved to absorb sound, perhaps as much as 25 per cent of the signal.

Up in the sky on this warm night, an ageless battle continues to rage.

WEEK 26

Dog-day cicada

Neotibicen canicularis

NORTH AMERICA; 27–33 mm (1¹⁄₁₆–1⅓ in), WINGSPAN 82 mm (5¼ in)

 YOU COULD SAY THAT THERE WERE two types of cicadas in North America – dog-day cicadas, and cicadas that dog the days of Americans.

The cicadas are a group of distinctive insects that belong to the order known as true bugs (Hemiptera). They are most famous for their songs, made by amorous males, which can create a wonderful atmosphere redolent of hot, humid weather. Over much of the world, their chirping is among the loudest made by any insect. Although it varies greatly, it is often similar to the sound made by a power saw, or a loud rattle. It is produced by a pair of special organs, the tymbals, which are ribbed membranes on the top of the front of the abdomen. Internal muscles contract and cause the tymbals to buckle inwards and, when the muscles relax, they pop back into

113

position to make the noise. Remarkably, much of the abdomen is hollow inside and acts as a soundbox to amplify the signal.

In North America, cicadas are often heard most in the 'dog days' of late summer and early autumn, when it is hot, sultry and sweaty and nobody wants to do anything. The term 'dog days' originally comes from the appearance of Sirius, the Dog Star. Somehow the noise of the cicadas just adds to the sense of inertia. The creatures making this song are various species in the genus *Neotibicen*, and they are often known as annual cicadas. They appear every year, and summer is not summer without them.

The annual cicadas usually spend three to five years underground as nymphs, sucking at plant roots. They emerge, moult into fairly substantial, winged adults and the males begin singing; mating occurs, the females lay eggs in living tree limbs and the nymphs fall back into the ground. Since broods overlap, they are always there but never overwhelming.

Although occurring almost throughout the continent, dog-day cicadas are not the only cicadas in North America. There are some that are much more celebrated (at least by entomologists), because they follow what must be one of the strangest life cycles of any animal on Earth. These are the periodical cicadas (genus *Magicicada*). An individual nymph hatches out and then returns to the earth, not to appear for a ridiculously long length of time – either 13 years (usually in the south) or 17 years (in the north).

When periodical cicadas hatch out, they do so rather locally (different broods hatch in different places in different years) and, literally, in their millions – for example, three million have been estimated in the area of a football pitch – all synchronized within a few days. Smaller than annual cicadas, and with red eyes and red in the wings, these bug-eyed beauties become a serious fact of life for the humans living near them. Although not especially loud individually, their chirping can be overwhelming, and people have suffered from damage to their hearing as a result; the sound can reach 100 decibels. Outdoor events sometimes have to be cancelled, even weddings, simply because the cicadas get everywhere, and people are unable to talk to each other above the din. When the bugs die, they have to be swept up and removed from back yards and driveways. They can truly dog the late-spring and midsummer days when they hatch out.

These extraordinary emergences beg two questions. *Why* do the periodical cicadas emerge in such bulk, and *how?* The first answer is that the vast numbers simply swamp their many predators and parasites. Cicadas make a good meal (some humans eat them), but if millions all hatch out at the same time, no enemies can possibly wipe them out. Indeed, the sound they make is so loud that their major enemies, birds, often ignore them. Why they live in the ground for 12 and 16 consecutive seasons is less obvious, but it might be to avoid the likelihood of predator adaptation; the figure of 13 or 17 years ensures that no predator with a regular life cycle is likely to follow suit.

Their chirping can be overwhelming, and people have suffered from damage to their hearing as a result; the sound can reach 100 decibels.

How, though, do they know when to emerge? After all, if the strategy goes wrong, it would be a catastrophe. The answer isn't known for sure, but it could be related to the changes in some internal chemical compounds. The cicadas may also be able to 'count' how many times the tree whose sap they are drinking produces flowers. However, the full truth isn't yet known. It is a truly remarkable mystery.

Common black ant

Lasius niger

ALMOST WORLDWIDE; 3–5 mm (⅛–¼ in), REPRODUCTIVE MALES UP TO
4.5 mm (⅙ in), QUEENS UP TO 9 mm (⅓ in)

IT'S A RARE MOMENT INDEED WHEN THE
weather forecast mentions insects. But every year,
an event occurs that affects so many people and
piques so much interest that it makes the bulletins.
It's often known as Flying Ant Day. It's the day
when the Lilliputians of our garden soil, patios, driveways and paths
suddenly take wing and impinge on our consciousness. Some people
are disgusted, afraid that the insects might have the temerity to get into
their hair or about their person – and sometimes they do, causing no
harm at all. Parents shut their children indoors, afraid of the apparent
apocalypse raging. Many other people are just curious, seeing the
plumes of insects rising from the ground, like reverse drizzle. The local
birds revel. A good sign that Flying Ant Day has arrived is the flocks of
birds mingling above rooftop height; they often include gulls, sparrows

and starlings as well as martins and swifts. For them, it is a bonanza of easy food. It is for spiders, too.

Flying Ant Day invariably occurs during warm weather; it is a summer event in Europe, from July to early September. It isn't always at the same time each year. In a given location, it usually occurs on a day without wind, and an improvement on the day before; it often takes place after rain. It is essential for the ants to be able to swarm, to gather above ground in large numbers without being whisked away by gusts of strong wind or dispersed too far away from each other. The whole idea of the day is for ants to meet and copulate.

Over much of Europe, common black ants inhabit the soil under rocks and roots and in rotting wood in farms, villages, towns and cities. They are the common ant that most of us see in the garden. They live in colonies that, on average, have about 5,000 workers, with a single queen that, remarkably, may live for more than 20 years. Every year, the colony embarks on an expansion project. The queen begins to produce unmated queens from fertilized eggs and males from unfertilized eggs. These, in contrast to the workers, have wings – they are technically known as alates. These are the individuals that will embark on the nuptial flights. Before their maiden voyages, they are greatly fussed over by the colony members.

Within hours, the whole festival is over, both for the ants and for their predators.

Whatever triggers the flight to begin, it has to be a common signal. There would be no point in one colony setting off its debutantes to a ball that has no other attendees. In a given local area, the colonies coordinate their take-offs, which is why Flying Ant Day is so spectacular. Millions of winged hopefuls rise into the air, into an orgy of mating, and also gene flow. The mixing ensures against inbreeding.

Once aloft, the flying queens and males get together and copulate in mid-air. The queens may indulge several suitors. Royalty will never mate again, but they gain enough sperm for the rest of their reproductive lives. Meeting above ground is, of course, enormously risky, but there are usually enough bodies to ensure that at least some mated queens survive. Within hours, the whole festival is over, both for the ants and for their predators.

Once they have mated, the males have served their purpose. They come to ground and may, if they are fortunate, live for a few more days before dying. In complete contrast, their mates may yet enjoy thousands of days of life.

The mated queens land and, if all has gone well, they have dispersed well away from their natal colony and will hope to start anew in a foreign land. The first thing they do is to bite off their own wings. They then set about finding a few square centimetres of soil where they might just squeeze into the neighbourhood as a new resident. They quickly produce new workers, and the colony is founded.

How many years could a queen survive, to know that it has been a success? It would have to look back on the day, my friend, when the ants were blowin' in the wind.

WEEK 28

Eastern tiger swallowtail

Papilio glaucus

EASTERN NORTH AMERICA; WINGSPAN 80–140 mm (5⅛–5½ in)

 IF YOU ARE A BUTTERFLY LOVER IN EUROPE and happen to pick up a field guide or app of North American butterflies, it's hard not to feel a tinge of envy. Look at all those swallowtails! In the UK, we just have one species and it's very rare, while in Europe there are only three or four. But in North America there are many (about 30) – zebra swallowtails, giant swallowtails and spicebush swallowtails, for instance – and several of them are common and widespread. It's a bit rich, in every sense.

For many Americans, the most familiar of these are the tiger swallowtails – eastern, western, Canadian and Appalachian. The first two are regular garden butterflies, the sort that you might also meet as you were driving along a highway, adorning the flowery verges, or on a visit to a park. Although they are very much treetop butterflies,

121

gliding above the canopy and laying their eggs there, they cannot resist coming down to our level, either to visit flowers for nectar or to indulge in the pursuit of mud-puddling. The latter involves these big, showy butterflies coming down to drink, often in 'clubs' (apparently only of males) when they pick up water, sodium, amino acids and other treats.

The tiger swallowtail is easily ushered into your own garden, if you provide plenty of nectar-producing flowers. Among its favourites are honeysuckle, milkweed, lilac, buddleia, bee-balm, thistles and black-eyed Susan. You can even add an elevated tray of moistened sand for the boys. You do not need to mount a special expedition to see these butterflies. They are so obvious that the eastern tiger swallowtail is the state butterfly of several states in the eastern USA. It was also the first butterfly to be drawn by European settlers, and by the naturalist John White in 1587.

The eastern tiger swallowtail lays its eggs in the canopy of large forest trees, including cottonwoods, tulip trees, cherries and magnolias. Each egg is laid singly on the upper side of a leaf. The early instar larvae live on mats of silk that they spin themselves, and later instars commute between these silken bedrooms and other nearby parts of the plant, which they eat. The final instar caterpillars are quite extraordinary. Each has prominent spots on the bulbous head, which look remarkably like eyes, and also possesses a remarkable organ, as do all swallowtails, called the osmeterium. When everted from the prothoracic segment it is fleshy, orange and forked, and looks very similar to the forked tongue of a snake. The resemblance is astonishing. The osmeterium also secretes noxious, foul-smelling fluids, so you would be a bold predator indeed to approach the larva.

Throughout most of its range, the eastern tiger swallowtail can be found in two forms, the 'normal' one with the yellow colour and black tiger stripes, and a 'black' one, which is essentially that – black above, with similar lines of outer yellow and blue spots to the paler individuals. They look like completely different species, although in the black morph, the yellow or cream is simply replaced by sooty black.

The intriguing part of this is that all the black morphs are female. In the reverse situation to ourselves, female butterflies have X and Y chromosomes, while males are homogametic, so the black morph is carried down the female line alone by a single gene. Throughout their range, all males are tiger-patterned. Bizarrely, the males' preferences are strongly in favour of pale morphs, which receive a greater level of male attention.

The black morphs, though, are better survivors, because they are mimics of another swallowtail species, the pipevine swallowtail (*Battus philenor*). The latter is a distasteful species avoided by predators. The tiger swallowtail is tasteful, but hides behind the appearance of the other species, the spicebush swallowtail (*Papilio troilus*) – another pipevine mimic, but a permanent one with no pale morph. It pays to have unattractive friends, it seems. These are classic example of Batesian mimicry, where an edible species evolves to resemble the inedible. In the north of their range, all the eastern tiger swallowtails are yellow, because the pipevine swallowtail is more of a southern species.

You do not need to mount a special expedition to see these butterflies. They are so obvious that the eastern tiger swallowtail is the state butterfly of several states in the eastern USA.

European stag beetle

Lucanus cervus

WESTERN EUROPE;
FEMALES 30–50 mm (1¼–2 in), MALES UP TO 75 mm (3 in)

THE EUROPEAN STAG BEETLE REALLY IS the stuff of legend. So-called because of the huge, antler-like appendages brandished by the males, the European stag beetle is one of the UK's largest insects, and certainly one of the most recognizable. These little leviathans are etched into the fabric of our wildlife landscape, even though the majority of us have never even seen one.

One of the reasons they are so elusive is that they are nocturnal and quite specific about emergence conditions. Warm, humid evenings in mid-June are a good time to start planning stag-spotting, but even then, they don't just appear everywhere. But they can appear almost *anywhere*. Surprisingly, the majority of British records come from the suburbs of London where there are good numbers of mature deciduous trees to harbour localized populations. On a balmy night, just after dusk, they appear seemingly from nowhere, as they emerge from the ground and climb, unseen, up tree trunks. Many an unwitting human has received the shock of their lives from being caught in the flight path of the noisy, unwieldy inaugural flight of a stag.

Adult European stag beetles' sole purpose upon emergence is to reproduce and disperse. Males quickly take to the wing, instinctively following the heady and irresistible pheromones of any nearby females. Several males will inevitably approach the same female, which can lead to fierce battles, where victory is invariably claimed with the stronger stag flinging the weaker adversary aside with those eponymous appendages. The males' antlers are in fact modified mandibles. However, the meaty apparatus serves no catering purpose because, unlike many of their beetle relatives, adult European stag beetles do not eat solid food. Their fleeting time above ground leaves time only to mate; eating is a wastefully superfluous task for the European stag beetle, save for occasionally licking sugary sap from tree bark or juices from decaying fruit.

On a balmy night, just after dusk, they appear seemingly from nowhere.

However, the transitory phase of the adult belies its 'other' existence. We think of this beetle as being short-lived; that its emergence is synonymous with its birth. But this could not be further from the truth. Its manifestation as an adult is an ephemeral swan song, serving only to complete the astonishingly long life cycle of this most enigmatic and impressive beast.

The life of any European stag beetle that you are lucky enough to see, began at least five years ago, beneath your feet. Eggs are laid in loose, loamy soil near dead wood, ideally a rotting broadleaf tree stump. The larvae are saproxylic (dependent on dead wood) and upon hatching burrow into the soft, decaying tree where they embark upon an 'all-you-can-eat' buffet. They will spend the next 5–7 years eating, growing and moulting, becoming colossal in size. The considerable fat reserves they build up are important, because they will expend a huge amount of energy during pupation, each transforming from a soft, squidgy larva into an armoured, winged colossus of a beetle – one of the true wonders of nature.

The soft, squidgy larva must maximize its chances of finding a mate by becoming as mobile as possible; this is where metamorphosis works its magic. Over just a few weeks, the simple-looking larva will completely transform into a complex, hard-shelled adult. It will then spend the winter underground, ready to emerge in late spring, fully equipped to fulfil the need to perpetuate its DNA.

Our increasing obsession with keeping things tidy and ordered is a direct threat to European stag beetle populations. The dead wood and rotting stumps that they require are too often removed to make way for paving and pristine lawns. Mature trees and orchards are cleared for redevelopment in urban areas, reducing the available habitat. Large numbers are killed by vehicles when they land on roads, attracted by the warm surface. Many are simply exterminated by humans fearful of their size and appearance. Such is the threat to European stag beetle numbers, that this remarkable beetle is now a legally protected species in the UK and is classed as a 'priority species', listed on Schedule 5 of the Wildlife and Countryside Act 1981.

Aphid

Family Aphididae

WORLDWIDE; 1–6 mm (UP TO ¼ in)

WE'VE ALL WATCHED IN DESPAIR AS, seemingly overnight, our favourite garden plant becomes the hot new place to be for a seething mass of aphids that have come to literally drink the place dry. It's hard to believe that a minuscule insect can create such havoc, but when it comes to aphids, the whole is truly greater than the sum of its parts. While one or two will cause barely a leaf to twitch, the subsequent thousands that inevitably follow can be a matter of life or death to a plant.

What makes the tiny aphid such a formidable adversary for the gardener? How on earth do they multiply so prodigiously? The answer is in an extraordinarily efficient reproductive lifestyle. Aphids can reproduce both sexually (male, female, sperm, egg) and asexually (clones), depending upon the conditions in which they find themselves.

Things are fairly conventional (in human terms) in late summer and early autumn; as temperatures start to drop, males emerge to mate with females, who then lay eggs that will overwinter in diapause. All this sounds fairly ... 'normal', so far, doesn't it? Well, things take a deliciously complex turn in spring as *all* the overwintered eggs hatch into females, and here's where things get even more interesting. Each of these females is already carrying her own young and within that unborn youngster is yet another germinal growth. This insect version of matryoshka nesting dolls (called parthengenesis) is the result of hormonal changes that give the female aphids the ability to reproduce asexually – there is no need to mate. They have, quite literally, cut out the middleman.

Nymphs mature quickly, which in itself is a useful tool for rapid reproduction. They will start producing their own young within 7–10 days of their own births but, in another stroke of evolutionary genius, the females give birth to *live young*, speeding up the reproductive process even further. So exponential is the birth rate (a single female can churn out up to 80 nymphs in a week), that a single aphid can be the source of billions of descendants in a single year. You may have heard the old saying 'breeding like rabbits', but it's fair to say that the reproductive prowess of bunnies is easily outmatched by these bugs.

Adult aphids are unable to survive colder winters, but they have yet another trick up their sleeves. In late summer, the females undergo another hormonal change and they begin to produce males. The females will now revert into egg-laying mode. But why lay eggs at all, when mass-producing clones is such a successful strategy? Unlike the adults, the eggs are cold-tolerant and able to survive through winter conditions that would kill off all the adults. Another advantage of this annual sexual reproduction is that it gives a little injection of genetic diversity to ensure that descendants can continually adapt to changes in conditions.

If all of this isn't impressive enough, females can also choose whether their young have wings. For example, if food resources are running low in a particular location, winged aphids are produced, which will then disperse to find a new food source. When it comes to reproductive success, aphids have nailed it. A combination of sexual reproduction and parthenogenesis allows for both genetic fitness and population expansion that surpasses most of the animal kingdom. It also helps to explain how your garden can become inundated with these sap-suckers in the blink of an eye.

When it comes to reproductive success, aphids have nailed it.

But wait, before you run for the pesticide spray, let's consider the benefits of allowing your garden to become an aphid playground. The spring boom in aphid numbers is timed almost perfectly with the hatching of many insectivorous birds, and this is no coincidence. We've watched sparrows, tits and finches gather on our feeders in the winter months, but during the breeding season they need to revert back to their wild diet, as their chicks cannot digest the foods we offer them. The bulk of many a hatchling diet comprises aphids – without them a nest will fail, so the more aphids you have in your garden, the better. Besides birds, aphids are a plentiful food source for spiders, other insects, amphibians, reptiles and mammals. Quite simply, the more aphids you have the more wildlife will come to eat them, and that equals a *lot* of free pest control. While aphids can be a pain in the neck, the long-term benefits of letting aphids amass are incalculable to the many species of birds and pollinators that eat them, filling our gardens with colour, life and song.

Common froghopper

Philaenus spumarius

EUROPE, NORTHERN AFRICA, ASIA,
INTRODUCED TO NORTH AMERICA; 6 mm (¼ in)

ONE OF THE MANY DELIGHTS OF ENTOMOLOGY is that so many small, common insects are truly extraordinary. Take the common froghopper or, as it is known in North America, the meadow spittlebug. Who could make up one of its major talents – proficiency in farting?

It's true, though, and you have probably seen the results of this ability during country hikes. Look down, especially after spring rain, and you can often see very white pieces of froth on vertical plant stems or leaf nodes. They look just like foamy spittle, and give rise to the name, in Europe at least, of 'cuckoo-spit'. You can easily imagine a bird flying over and depositing its spit in such places. During the time when folk knew that the cuckoo didn't make a nest, but were ignorant of the details, it was thought that the spittle contained the embryo of the bird.

A quick look reveals that the inhabitant of the spittle is not a bird but a tiny insect, the nymph of the common froghopper. But what is the spittle for and how is it made? Well, it is created largely for protection – after all, the foam does not look appetizing, is somewhat acrid and isn't easily recognizable to a predator as food. It also keeps its inhabitant moist. And it is made by the bug placing its mouthparts into the xylem, the main artery of a plant stem. The xylem transports water under pressure, in a similar way to the mains supply delivered to a house, or water along a hose. By tapping into it using its sharp rostrum, the nymph ensures that sticky sap flows under pressure through its body. Two finger-like projections at the base of the abdomen blow air into the sap that has passed through the body, and the result is the nymph's curious coating of foam.

That isn't the only surprising talent of the froghopper. Its other claim to fame is its ability to jump. Many people are familiar with these diminutive plant bugs and know that they are able to spring away from danger, as if powered by a slingshot. But how well has only been discovered recently in the laboratory.

That isn't the only surprising talent of the froghopper. Its other claim to fame is in its ability to jump.

It turns out that the froghopper is the best jumper, relative to its own body length, in the entire insect world. It can spring more than 100 times its own height, which is equivalent to a human jumping over a tall building, such as a tower. Individuals just 6 mm (¼ in) long were able to clear 70 cm (27½ in), which is more than enough to take them from one plant to another. They easily outperform fleas, which were the previous world-record holders.

While the bald facts are impressive, a closer look at the mechanics shows how extraordinary this is. A froghopper's leap encompasses an acceleration from nothing to a speed of 4 m/sec (13 ft/sec) within a time interval of a single millisecond! That's an acceleration of 4,000 m/sec² (13,000 ft/sec²). The G-force involved is 400 times that of gravity. When humankind has gone into space, astronauts sometimes experience a G-force of 5 – which shows that we are but amateurs.

This extraordinary performance is generated by nothing more than the froghopper's hindlegs. They are longer than the other four and are dragged along somewhat awkwardly if a froghopper crawls. But, if it is about to jump, its hindlimbs are held cocked by a series of ridges on the exoskeleton. This tension adds to the contraction of the muscles and, once the spring-loaded legs move out of the ridges, away the froghopper flies.

It only goes to show that wildlife marvels can be found close to home. Who knows what other invertebrate talents remain hidden under our noses?

Hummingbird hawk-moth

Macroglossum stellatarum

EUROPE, CENTRAL ASIA AND NORTHERN AFRICA;
WINGSPAN 40–50 mm (1½–2 in)

HOW LOVELY TO BE SITTING IN YOUR garden or local park, absorbing the balmy heat of late afternoon in high summer. Insects buzz around the flowers, resting on them to gorge on pollen, or swoop briefly into flower heads to siphon nectar. Suddenly, out of the corner of your eye, you see something quite different. You think it's a bumblebee, until you realize it is hovering, like a drone suspended in mid-air. It zips diagonally to a flower then retreats backwards just as quickly to once more hover and survey. Your brain tells you it's a hummingbird, but it can't be, as you're in entirely the wrong continent and, besides, it doesn't even have a beak. What on earth *is* it? You have, in fact, just spotted one of our most fabulous and unique day-flying moths – the hummingbird hawk-moth.

Of the 160,000 species of moths in the world, the vast majority fly at night, which is a shame for us humans because we miss out on an extraordinary amount of diversity. Luckily for us, there are a good number of day-flying species, which allow us a brief glimpse into the life of the moth. Their diurnal cousins, the butterflies, are generally bigger, bolder and brighter, whereas many daytime moths are small and cryptic, to avoid detection. Some have bold warning colours to deter predators, but largely they all conform to roughly the same 'design' blueprint. It is doubtful, however, as to whether anybody remembered to send the evolutionary uniform memo to the hummingbird hawk-moth, and so it decided to do its own thing. The result is the likely outcome of asking a child to draw a gerbil with wings. More mammalian than arthropod in appearance, the dense fuzz and large, round eyes – each with a soulful 'pseudo-pupil' – make it look like a baby rodent, and yet it flies strongly with wings that function more like a hummingbird's than a moth's, allowing it to fly in any direction and hold a static position to observe its surroundings. It also feeds like a hummingbird, using an extremely long proboscis (in place of a tongue) to probe into elongated, tubular flowers, such as valerian, verbena, jasmine and buddleia.

At rest it is a fairly unremarkable moth, a uniform grey-brown colour from above with few distinguishing features – an effective camouflage strategy. In flight, however, things are very different; as the wings beat, the orange hindwing and underneath of the forewing are visible, creating a striking, tangerine blur in the sunshine. Its abdomen has a feathery fringe bearing a black and white pattern that resembles a tail and only adds further to the avian illusion of this most enigmatic creature.

The hummingbird hawk-moth is a moth of many feats: in flight its wings beat at around 85 beats per second, and it is thought to reach speeds of up to 19 km/h (12 mph). Its proboscis is approximately the same length as its body – around 25 mm (1 in). It is present across much of Europe, North Africa and Central Asia, and each summer many individuals will undertake the journey north-west, across continental Europe and the English Channel on to the UK and Ireland, where it can be seen from late spring if the temperatures are mild and dry. In warmer climates, the hummingbird hawk-moth will overwinter as an adult; historically the winters of more northerly regions have been too cold for it to survive, but recently there have been reports of individuals successfully overwintering in the UK – an indicator of climate change as average minimum temperatures continue to rise. The hummingbird hawk-moth may be one of a number of species to benefit from climatic shift, expanding its breeding potential northwards, and there is no doubt that it is a hugely welcome and exotic sight when it suddenly appears around our flower-filled gardens, courtyards and balconies.

It is doubtful, however, as to whether anybody remembered to send the evolutionary uniform memo to the hummingbird hawk-moth, and so it decided to do its own thing.

WEEK 33

Marmalade hoverfly

Episyrphus balteatus

EUROPE, NORTHERN ASIA AND NORTHERN AFRICA;
9–12 mm (UP TO ½ in)

TAKE A MOMENT OR TWO TO SPARE A
thought for the humble marmalade hoverfly, for it is
overlooked in many ways. The perennial pollinator
bridesmaid, it watches quietly from the front pew
as the bee gets all the attention for its services to
flowering plants. It stands in the wings of the pest-control stage as the
ladybird takes the spotlight. And it quietly flies under the radar as we
marvel at the seasonal flight accomplishments of migratory birds. And
yet its quiet demeanour belies a truly heroic insect. Let me tell you a
little about this anything-but-ordinary fly.

To say that the marmalade hoverfly is understated is, well, an
understatement. It is of slight build, with a delicate body of muted
orange, with alternating thick and thin, black, horizontal stripes;
sometimes it is seen in a darker, melanistic variation. It has large,

clear wings that are held at a 45-degree angle, like a shallow isosceles triangle. Whereas many hoverflies are quite noisy in flight, the marmalade is a discreet presence, silently going about its business of nectaring, eating pollen and seeking out potential partners. You really wouldn't know it was there.

So large are some migratory groups that they can be detected on radar.

The marmalade hoverfly begins to make an appearance in mid-spring, although it can be seen earlier, on those anomalously warm, sunny days of late winter. These individuals are the toughest members of the small, resident population that survives overwintering; shorter winters are thought to increase their chances of success. Come late spring, numbers increase significantly and, while a number of these individuals are still emerging from brumal dormancy, the majority have just completed one of the most remarkable migrations of any species on Earth.

One of our most prolific migrators, the marmalade hoverfly begins its life at either end of Europe, depending on its place of birth. A spring generation will begin its life in the southern Mediterranean or northern Africa, and then set out northward, across continental Europe. Around *4 billion* individuals will make this journey, flying at altitudes between 150 m (500 ft) and 1 km (⅔ mile) over distances of around 2,500 km (1,500 miles); they have even been discovered flying through the Alps. So large are some migratory groups that they can be detected on radar. Arrival at their destinations significantly swells local populations. At intervals along the migratory route, they will make rest stops where they feed, and seek out colonies of aphids among which the females lay their eggs, for while the adults are vegetarian, the larvae that emerge are insatiable insectivores that will immediately set to work, eating their way through their primary food source, which just happens to be aphids. The transit of such large numbers of hoverflies across the continent results in the consumption of vast numbers of aphids, thus making them one of the most important contributors to ecosystem services in Europe, for their roles in pest control and pollination. Research shows that well-timed broods significantly increase cereal crop yield along migratory routes, simply because the larvae are so effective at controlling local aphid numbers. There is also a marked increase in food for predators higher up the food chain; this flying buffet benefits many animals such as birds and bats along the way.

The life cycle of a non-overwintering adult is relatively short – around one month – meaning that multiple generations occur over the breeding season. As the end of summer approaches, the late-generation hoverflies pack up and head south again. A successful breeding season means that the number heading south will exceed the amount that arrived in spring. What is truly extraordinary is that no hoverfly flies both ways. Migration is undertaken using only instinct, in-built GPS and air currents to find the way back across Europe to warmer winter climes. All this, in an insect that measures around 1cm (just under ½in) in length and weighs around 0.01g (a tiny fraction of an ounce).

This incredible hoverfly really is the unsung superhero of our gardens.

True katydid

Pterophylla camellifolia

NORTH AMERICA; UP TO 50 mm (2 in)

WE NEED TO TALK ABOUT KATY. SOME SAY she did, and some say she didn't, and there is an argument raging.

The 'dispute' is between male bush-crickets.

During the hot summer nights in the eastern side of North America, you can hear them calling, first one cohort and then another, up in the trees. One cohort calls 'Katy-did', by rubbing its forelegs together, and all the cohort agrees in unison. The other cohort calls 'Katy-didn't', also in unison, and so they go on all night, each cohort alternating. The 'Katy-did' and 'Katy-didn't' resounding chorus, already heated by the warm night, can hot up so much that the sound is almost deafening. It certainly alarmed the early European settlers.

Traditionally, there is no backing down, as you can tell from this poem by a certain Oliver Wendell Holmes, writing in 1831:

'I love to hear thine earnest voice,
Wherever thou art hid,
Thou testy little dogmatist,
Thou pretty Katydid!'

And so there shouldn't be. Each male true katydid is calling to a
potential mate, and mating is a serious business. There is intense
competition, and the sheer effort put in by males to ensure pairing
is successful is astonishing. Bush-crickets are among the very few
groups of insects that, when they copulate, present a nuptial gift in
addition to their sperm. The spermatophore passed to the female
contains the ampulla, which is the bit that actually contains the sperm,
plus a gelatinous goo bursting with protein, which is known as the
spermatophylax. The spermatophore remains available to the female
after mating, and she duly eats both parts. However, she consumes the
spermatophylax first, and it has been suggested that its function is to
ensure that the female doesn't eat the ampulla until it is entirely empty
of sperm. Alternatively, the food package almost certainly helps the
female in egg development and may increase the number of eggs.
The spermatophylax is an enormous investment, amounting to about
40 per cent of the male's body weight. So, let's hope Katy did well.

Although this bush-cricket is famous for its call, the loud rasping
varies greatly throughout the range of the true katydid, from the Great
Lakes down to Texas, and by no means all males make the 'Katy-did'
call. Some populations are slower than others or have different rates of
chirping. The northern true katydids have a slow pulse rate and utter
2–4 pulses per chirp. The south-western ones are also slow and utter
only 1–2 pulses per chirp. Things buck up in the south-east, with males
giving 3–5 pulses per chirp. And then things go completely mad in,
of all places, Iowa. Here the racy males can give as many as 15 pulses

per chirp. At first, these differences suggest that four separate species might be involved, but intermediates are regularly found in the contact zones between populations, suggesting uninhibited gene flow.

However familiar the call might be, most people have never seen a katydid. It is very much a browser in the treetops, occurring in both deciduous and conifer tree crowns, and its leaf-green colouration hides it well. In fact, rather little is known about it at all. Both males and females have large wings, but they fly very poorly, relying on gliding to get from tree to tree.

However familiar the call might be, most people have never seen a katydid.

Without its distinctive call, the katydid would be a member of the vast tribe of overlooked insects.

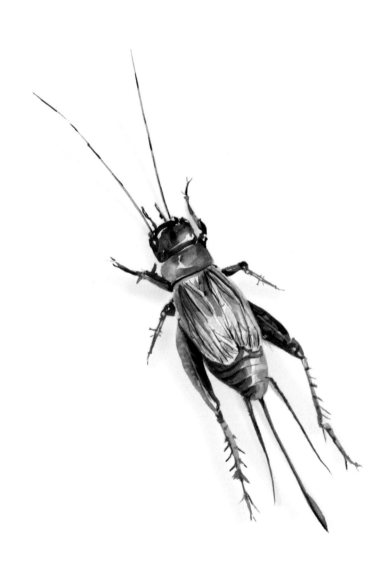

Fall field cricket

Gryllus pennsylvanicus

NORTH AMERICA; 15–25 mm (½–1 in)

 WHICH ANIMAL HAS CONTRIBUTED TO MORE movies or TV shows than any other, apart from humans? The answer could well be the cricket, the ultimate voiceover artist. Whenever a director requires a wild track to evoke the night, especially a summer night in North America, there can be nothing better than the gentle, soothing and persistent call of the fall field cricket or its close relative the spring field cricket (*Gryllus veletis*). These insects should have been credited literally thousands of times.

The fall field cricket is a familiar garden neighbour over most of North America except the dry south-west. Sometimes it is a little too familiar, settling comfortably into houses and calling from indoors, in utility rooms, under sinks and even inside cupboards. It starts chirping as dusk falls and will then carry on unbroken throughout the night. On warm, sultry nights, when it is difficult to sleep anyway, a lullaby from an indoor cricket can be a mixed blessing.

The sound is made by the cricket rubbing its forewings together. There is a 'scraper' on one forewing, and this is oriented so that it can be rubbed across a set of teeth on the other forewing. The number of teeth varies between all the cricket species, so that each song is different to other local species and is identifiable. Fall field crickets make three calls: a long-distance chirp that attracts females from a distance; another chirp to use during close courtship; and a third to fight off rivals that have come too close.

Studies have shown that female fall field crickets listen to the calls of males very intently and can assess them without the need to meet up. This long-distance assessment is useful, because in the wild the singing males are often quite far apart, usually 7–10 m (23–33 ft). For an insect that doesn't fly, this isn't a short hop. The females listen carefully to how many syllables there are, the rate of calling and many other cues. Females greatly prefer older males, regardless of any other characteristics. An experiment found that males that were 15 or more days past their moult into adulthood were of far greater interest than males only 7–9 days old.

Each song is different to other local species and is identifiable.

Unfortunately, female fall field crickets aren't the only listeners to the male's songs. The sounds also lure a fly called *Ormia*, which does not have the performer's interests at heart. It is a parasitoid, which lays first-instar larvae on the body of the cricket; these burrow into the unfortunate animal's muscle and essentially eat it from the inside, killing it quite slowly. What is extraordinary is how the fly finds its host; it must hear it and be able to pinpoint its position accurately.

Its ears, though, are too close together to use the method most ears do, which is to compute a time interval between the signal arriving between one ear and the other. Instead, the ears are effectively joined together in the cuticle, mechanically coupling them and magnifying the inter-aural time difference. New microphones have been designed using this unique system. Perhaps one day, moviemakers will use these novel microphones to record the songs of crickets, which would be a delicious irony.

Providing that all goes well, the field crickets mate and the female lays eggs into the soil, usually about 50 at a time. The season is already late, and these eggs will enter into winter diapause by October. The neighbourhood goes quiet, and even those people who might have had their nights disturbed, might find themselves feeling nostalgic for their summer whispers.

Ivy bee

Colletes hederae

EUROPE; 10–13 mm (²⁄₅–½ in)

AUTUMN IS A BITTERSWEET TIME IN THE entomological calendar. As the days grow shorter and the night air takes on a distinct nip, the number of insects declines significantly, especially of the flying type. By now, the majority of bugs and minibeasts have completed their life cycles. Many die, others hibernate, and a surprising number retreat into hiding places to overwinter. The warmer autumn days coax a range of flies, grasshoppers and bugs into the sunlight to catch the ebbing rays of our closest star. The last thing we would expect then, during summer's last act, is a mass emergence of bees – but we know by now that there is no 'usual' in the invertebrate world.

The ivy bee has been around for around 50 million years, and yet it was only described as a species in 1993, having hitherto been lumped in with a similar sister species of the same genus for a few hundred years. A smart-looking bee, the honey-bee-sized females have a short, buff pile across the thorax and broad, orangey-yellow stripes on the abdomen; the males are smaller and fluffier. Like many other solitary bees, they develop underground in 'aggregations' – large nesting sites of self-contained brood chambers with entrance holes packed tightly together; the bee equivalent of an apartment block. What is so special about the ivy bee, however, is how late it appears in the year, and how short a window it uses to reproduce. While other bees are emerging early to exploit spring sunshine and early nectar sources, the ivy bees are snugly tucked up in their underground nests. They are waiting for a particular flower to emerge – an unlikely hero of autumn which, thanks to its late blooming, has a more off-peak vibe than the high-summer nectar fest, a niche that the ivy bee uses fully to its advantage.

Ivy-bee season can begin as early as late August, when the males begin to appear; just a few at first, they emerge, find a nearby nectar source and then basically hang out near their nest entrances, awaiting the appearance of the females. In the UK, this begins to happen on a hot, sunny day around the first or second week of September. By this time, the number of males on the ground has swelled considerably and, after waiting for days, even weeks, for their chance to continue their gene pool, they are fervent to say the least. The first females to exit the access tunnels are radiating pheromones and barely make it into the light before they are covered by delirious, desperate males. It's literally every man for himself as they pile in, abdomens probing furiously as they attempt to lock on to her. The writhing mass becomes a moving lump – a 'mating ball' – rolling around on the ground with the female trapped somewhere in the middle. Once she has mated she breaks free of the mêlée and makes off to the nearest patch of ivy, leaving behind one successful male and plenty more disappointed. Unsurprisingly, ivy makes up the bulk of this bee's nectar intake, although it is known to have broadened its palate to other flowers such as dandelion and hawkbit. Once a female has fuelled up, she sets off to find a suitable place to lay her eggs.

Ivy bees are choosy about where they nest. Large, open areas of exposed, sandy soil are ideal, and females will often return to their birthplaces to build new brood chambers, or even reuse old ones. The brood chamber is where the magic really happens, because ivy bees are plasterer bees, and they have this name because of the ingenious way in which they protect their young. From a gland in the abdomen, close to the ovipositor, a transparent, cellophane-type substance is secreted, which the female bee then mixes with another substance from a salivary gland, creating a polymer. She applies – or 'plasters' – this polymer in a thin layer to the wall of the nest cell using her short, broad tongue, which characterizes the genus. She then stocks it with ivy pollen, lays an egg and seals the cell up with more of her wonder stuff. This substance effectively moisture-seals the egg and ivy-pollen provisions, protecting against mould growth and even flooding, and creating a stable microclimate for the egg and resulting larva to develop within for the next 11 months.

They develop underground in 'aggregations' ... the bee equivalent of an apartment block.

This new visitor to our shores was first recorded only in 2001, and has already reached Scotland, a feat possible due to the abundance of ivy in the British Isles. It might be worth leaving that old stand of ivy at the bottom of the garden; it could become a vital food source for one of our most intriguing and charismatic new residents.

Black and yellow garden spider

Argiope aurantia

NORTH AND CENTRAL AMERICA;
MALES 5–9 mm (⅕–¼ in) FEMALES 19–28 mm (¾–1 in)

AS THE NORTH-AMERICAN HIGH SUMMER TIPS gently into early autumn, the sun casts an ever-paler glow, pulling the shadows into long, abstract shapes in our gardens. This is the time of the black and yellow garden spider, which has arrived to create her own striking work of art in your back yard.

She can be an alarming sight; a large, ovoid spider with yellow and black transverse stripes that have earned her European cousin *Argiope bruennichi* the common name of wasp spider. Fear not. This outfit, although distinctly waspish, is merely a cunning device to deter predators, for she is a benign soul who is interested only in building her web and providing for her children.

The black and yellow garden spider belongs to the Araneidae family of orb-weaver spiders, which are famous for creating beautiful, concentric, circular webs, in the centre of which they sit patiently waiting for their food to come to them. These intricate webs are created by making radial lines like the spokes on a bicycle wheel. These are used as anchor points to stabilize the web, around which the sticky concentric spiral is plotted. The result is the perfect web typical of the orb-weavers, but the *Argiope* spiders don't stop there – they add an ingenious little extra which remains one of the wonderful mysteries of nature. A long, fuzzy, zig-zag of silk, called a stabilimentum, is 'drawn' downwards, from the centre to the lower margin of the web. Why? Well, here is where we lament our woeful inability to communicate with animals, because although the spiders know exactly what purposes this silky adornment serves, we, alas, do not. We have made a few guesses, mind you. For example, the stabilimentum could be a camouflage aid to help break up the outline of the spider as it sits in the web, or it could help to attract prey. It may actually make the web more visible to prevent larger animals from damaging it, in the same way that we put stickers on our windows to avoid bird strikes. It could also be a very forthright 'come hither' signal for potential mates. It is probably not an architectural device, as the silk zig-zag sits on top of the scaffold, rather than being built into it. We just don't know exactly what it's for and so, for now, it remains one of those glorious mysteries of the natural world. This fuzzy graffiti has earned this spider another common name: writing spider, because of the construction's similarity to a signature. Like most orb-weavers, the black and yellow garden spider has three claws on her 'foot' (other spider families have two);

One of the wonderful mysteries of nature – a long, fuzzy, zig-zag of silk, called a stabilimentum.

the third claw helps with manipulating the silk threads when spinning those large, intricate structures.

As with most spider unions, that of the black and yellow garden spider is fraught with danger, for the male anyway, for whom there is a terrifying size difference. He can be around a quarter of the size of his partner – quite the conjugal conundrum. A cautious, reverent approach is key to the male's success, if not survival. If he can successfully pass on his own unique genes to the next generation then his work is done; staying alive is merely a bonus. He just needs to make all the right moves at the right time, and at the right speed, and she will allow him to pass his sperm to her – then it's job done. In the likely event that he becomes the postcoital meal, he has at least provided an easy and highly nutritious meal to kickstart the development of his future offspring.

Upon receipt of the male's sperm, the female's parenting instincts now kick in, and she showcases another of her creative talents, forming a large, amphora-shaped sac into which she will deposit her eggs. The sac looks like the work of a paper wasp, but is actually formed from her silk. Her multiple spinnerets have several settings to suit different purposes. The fragile, papery cocoon is lined with fluffed-up silk to keep her babies warm and dry until they hatch, and it is attached to vegetation using those familiar, strong anchor lines.

There can be little doubt that the black and yellow garden spider is one of our most visually stunning back-yard visitors; a supercharged knitting machine mama whose appearance makes early autumn all the more colourful and compelling.

Monarch butterfly

Danaus plexippus

NORTH AND CENTRAL AMERICA, AUSTRALASIA AND THE
PACIFIC ISLANDS; WINGSPAN 90–100 mm (4 in)

NORTH AMERICA IS FAMOUS FOR ITS FALL
colours, but before the golds, reds and purples
appear in their marvellous magnificence in the
forests of the north, there is an outbreak of orange.
Catch a movement in the corner of your eye and
you might mistake it for a falling leaf, but this orange phenomenon is a
butterfly and, in common with the autumn colours, it moves south with
the season. This is the monarch, butterfly migration royalty.

The monarch's long journey is now one of the world's most celebrated
animal movements, eventually taking many millions of individuals to
a few high-altitude forests in central Mexico. (Monarchs west of the
Rockies go to the coast of California instead.) But at its beginning, it is
surprisingly subtle. You might just go out to hang the washing and find
that your garden zinnias are suddenly awash with the fiery-coloured

travellers, or there is a monarch at a stray patch of goldenrod in a mall car park. You don't see clouds of butterflies moving, darkening the sky; it's just that they are everywhere.

Only occasionally does the flow of gossamer wings become something more spectacular. At Cape May in New Jersey, for instance, I have seen streams of butterflies hurrying south over the marshes and dunes, an incredible lepidopteran rush-hour, bright amber seeing a green light. Here, in season, researchers monitor monarchs per hour.

In the north of their range, around the Great Lakes and the Maritime Provinces of Canada, these butterflies begin their migration as the days become shorter in August. Day length and slightly colder nights trigger the autumn generation of butterflies to put aside all thoughts of breeding, and to beginning their surge south. On days when the wind is northerly, they use the tail wind, and on still days they rise with the warm currents. Where there is an opposing southerly wind, they pause and devote themselves to drinking nectar for as long as daylight allows. A butterfly moving from its northern range will have increased its fatty fuel deposits by 500 per cent by the time it reaches Texas, all of it achieved by drinking from the very flowers that you might have planted on your own patch. It is humbling to think that a monarch residing in Mexico might have a few molecules of fuel from the filling stations outside your back door.

And so, they inch south, taking the summer with them. They are on the move for several months, arriving at the Gulf Coast of the USA in October and Mexico by December. It's a long way for an insect, up to 3,000 km (1,900 miles), and there is also a puzzle about how they find their way. Scientists think that they use a solar compass to know which way is south in autumn; the compass is probably found in the brain, while the necessary corrections according to the time of day are made by the antennae. Amazingly, the switch to following a northerly route after their hibernation is controlled by the cold temperatures they experience in Mexico.

While the migration of the monarch butterflies is famous, their winter torpor is perhaps even more staggering. Billions of butterflies descend onto an area of highland forest at 3,200 m (10,500 ft), higher than any of these travellers have been in their lifetimes. From an area of 2.6 million sq. km (1 million sq. miles), the eastern monarch population has funnelled into an area 30 km by 60 km (19 miles by 37 miles). Here the butterflies cluster on to every branch, every stem and every leaf, clothing the forest in a different kind of fall colour.

It takes the spring equinox to usher them from their diapause and urge these same individuals north again. Our eastern populations move north to the Gulf States, until they reach their own individual goals, the first of the spring flush of milkweed flowers. The females lay eggs and, after their journey of up to about 5,000 km (3,100 miles), they die.

An incredible lepidopteran rush-hour, bright amber seeing a green light.

In May, the spring generation heads north once more and – depending on where you are in North America – you will once again see monarchs in your summer garden. And the oddest thing is this. The summer individuals don't migrate at all, they just potter around your back yard. Migration? What migration?

Red imported fire ant

Solenopsis invicta

SOUTH AMERICA AND INTRODUCED TO NORTH AMERICA;

2.5–6 mm (UP TO ¼ in)

OF THE TWO HUNDRED OR SO SPECIES OF fire ant currently described around the world, the most famous – or infamous – species must surely be the South American fire ant, also known as the red imported fire ant. It is small and, unsurprisingly, red in colour with a squarish head and powerful, toothed mandibles. Originating on the South American continent, it has spread northwards into the southern USA since the early 20th century with great success, and the effects of climate change will only see it move further north over the coming decades. And although we may be suffering the effects of this accidental tourist's intrusion into our lives, we must remember that we only have ourselves to blame; exports of tropical fruit and plants along international trade routes have fast-tracked this fire ant to virtually all corners of America. Its success is partly due to the lack of natural predators in its new-found territories, which has allowed new populations to increase rapidly. It has also learned to live near humans, with colonies setting up home in what, to them, are fabulously suitable meadowlands and fields, but are quite often parks, gardens and paddocks, where nests can easily be sat on, kicked or trampled, unleashing a chain reaction of retaliation that invariably ends in tears and antihistamines. The fire ant has acquired its fearsome reputation by way of its propensity to attack aggressively and unwaveringly in the face of threat, with a sting potent enough to register on the Schmidt Sting Pain Index. It is described by the index's creator as 'sharp, sudden, mildly alarming. Like walking across a shag carpet and reaching for the light switch', and although it may only register as 1 out of 5 on the scale, the sheer number of fire ants likely to be stinging at one time as part of a coordinated offensive would probably break the strongest of constitutions.

Nests can easily be sat on, kicked or trampled, unleashing a chain reaction of retaliation that invariably ends in tears and antihistamines.

While we may lament the pointy end of the fire ant, let us also reflect on how important this ant is to other species. Their colonies are huge; it is estimated that a single hectare (2.5 acres) of meadow can produce up to a quarter of a million queens per year, so imagine how much food that is for myriad flying predators, such as martins, swifts, small raptors and dragonflies. On the ground, fire ants are hunted by animals of every shape and size, from spiders, lizards and antlions to armadillos, anteaters and woodpeckers. They play a critical role in the food web, although this may be hard to imagine, as we don't eat them ourselves (yet). Speaking of food, fire ants have a varied diet, which is useful when food is scarce. As with many other ant species, they will farm honeydew-bearing insects, such as aphids. They have been observed feeding on oozing tree sap and chewing on bark to the extent that irreversible damage is inflicted upon the tree. They will also feed on carrion – usually invertebrates, but sometimes larger animals, such as birds and mice.

They are resourceful homemakers too. Besides inhabiting the more traditional 'anthill', fire ants are one of several species that can live nomadically. The colony will move around freely and, when required, cluster together, linking legs – like a game of 'barrel of monkeys' – to create a tent-like construction called a bivouac, with workers making up the outer layer, protecting the queen, eggs and larvae within. Should the bivouac be inundated with water, it becomes a buoyant mass that floats on the surface – a significant advantage when searching for new territory as the ant-y 'lifeboat' can be carried great distances at speed that couldn't possibly be attained on tarsi. The workers that form the hull of this ant-ark are in direct contact with the water and obviously at greatest risk. Their waterproof exoskeletons help to keep the raft afloat, and tiny hairs on their bodies trap a thin layer of air to allow them to 'breathe' for a short time through the spiracles along their bodies; workers will regularly rotate buoyancy duty to keep the ship sailing. Once the waters recede and the ants are back on *terra firma*, the raft is dismantled and they will set about finding an ideal patch of ground to settle the colony, and with a hell of a story to tell the kids.

Foam grasshopper

Dictyophorus spumans

SOUTHERN AFRICA; UP TO 80 mm (3⅛ in)

GRASSHOPPERS ARE SPRING-LOADED SUMMER insects. Few other invertebrates, except butterflies and, to some extent bees, are appreciated more by humankind. Many of us treasure memories spent lying in the long grass on hot days, accompanied by the cheery chirping of these animals – a sound, incidentally, produced by rubbing comb-like pegs on the hindlegs against the forewings (unlike crickets – see page 148). Children adore approaching grasshoppers and watching them spring away, an experience of wonder and delight, and at times anyone walking through long grass will witness some impressive escape-leaps. There is a genuine feeling of optimism in their vivacity, a sense that we are encountering a more carefree world. One of Aesop's fables is known as *The Ants and the Grasshopper*, and the crux of the story is that the ant works and strives hard all summer long, while the grasshopper treats life with perilous abandon. The ant prepares for winter and survives, while the grasshopper comes to grief.

This isn't quite true, although it's close. Although individual workers don't last the whole year, ant colonies do indeed survive all year round and the queens are long-lived. The grasshopper, on the other hand, in common with most insects, has an annual cycle of a few months and passes its life on to the next stage, its eggs laid in the soil. These overwinter until the earth reaches a certain temperature, upon which the first instar hatches, which is a true miniature compared to the adult. It usually moults about six times before attaining full adult size.

What is most extraordinary about the foam grasshopper is just how defensive it is ... Any animal that persists beyond this point deserves everything it gets.

Grasshoppers, often abundant, are prey to many species, from spiders to birds. In some parts of the world, for instance in Mexico, China and parts of Africa, they are eaten by people too. It might well be that this habit grows, since insects are both nutritious and, by all accounts, tasty.

However, one grasshopper which most definitely won't find its way on to any menu, whether human or otherwise, is the gorgeous foam grasshopper, a species from southern Africa, which occurs in scrub, parks and gardens, especially in the mountains. This particular species breaks many grasshopper conventions, not least being brilliantly coloured. It is also polymorphic, showing off a range of colours and patterns wherever it occurs.

What is most extraordinary about the foam grasshopper is just how defensive it is, a far cry from the grasshopper's carefree image. The extreme brightness of the colouration is a sure sign that that it is unpalatable, a signal known as aposematicism. It is backed up by body fluids that are indeed not just unpalatable but potentially harmful. The foam grasshopper is unusually fussy for eschewing most vegetation in favour of consuming a small range of poisonous plants, notably milkweeds (the monarch butterfly and the milkweed leaf beetle, see pages 160 and 72, do the same), thereby downloading their chemical defences. These toxins, which are cardiac glycosides, have been known to be fatal to dogs.

You might think that the foam grasshopper has made its point, but clearly the predators of southern Africa are persistent. If this animal is threatened, it secretes an unpleasant-looking foam that is also noxious. And if this still isn't enough, the foam grasshopper will also make a hissing sound. Any animal that persists beyond this point deserves everything it gets.

As a result of these bulletproof defences, the foam grasshopper can move across the ground with relative impunity, not at any great pace.

In fact, it barely even hops!

Common green lacewing

Chrysoperla carnea

EUROPE; 10 mm (⅖ in)

THE COMMON GREEN LACEWING IS EASY enough to identify; a long, slender, lime-green body with large, transparent, swept-back wings that are held in a tent shape over the body. It is a delicate little soul, and distinctive too. But to truly appreciate this splendid creature, you need to get very close, because then you can fully appreciate the astonishingly rainbow-coloured, hemispherical compound eyes that gleam like polished opals. You will also see the exquisite details of the wings: a latticework of veins so intricate that the finest stained-glass window maker would be proud to claim as their own.

These little sprites are largely crepuscular or nocturnal and can often be seen on warm summer nights; tiny emerald intruders attracted through open doors into our brightly lit buildings that could be mistaken for exotic moths. Lacewings are entirely harmless – they do not bite or sting us, nor do they seek out our food. The adults, predominantly nectar- and honeydew-feeders, spend the few weeks of their final life stages on the wing, eating, mating and becoming food for many other animals.

The female has an ingenious method for protecting her eggs from predators: as she lays each egg, she attaches it to a sticky mucus that is stretched into a long, thin thread and fixed to the underside of a leaf or similar substrate. Many eggs can be deposited together, with the average female laying 100–200 eggs in her adult phase, which lasts 4–6 weeks. The mucus filament hardens, leaving the egg suspended, seemingly in mid-air, like a tiny bauble on a Christmas tree. In some species, the filament is coated with a chemical to repel ants; another cunning ploy that keeps the egg safe from predators. Or at least it *should*, except there is one predator that the lacewing hasn't accounted for – itself.

Cannibalism is common practice in these animals, and it is every lacewing for itself.

While the adult may be sweetness and light, its children are an entirely different matter. The moment it breaks free from its lofty egg case, the common green lacewing larva is an eating machine. It is rather like a pudgy, flattened caterpillar, although it is in possession of large, curved mouthparts. It will literally eat the first thing it can lay those pincers on, which is often one of its siblings; cannibalism is common practice in these animals, and it is every lacewing for itself from the get-go. Eating one's siblings is but temporary opportunism; the lacewing's preferred diet is soft-bodied invertebrates, such as scale insects and mites, and a large quantity of aphids. So enthusiastic is its appetite for these tiny sap-suckers, that the lacewing has earned the nickname 'aphid lion' and has become a significant asset to biological warfare in the agricultural sector, as its efficiency in controlling populations of 'pest' species becomes increasingly recognized as the natural alternative to chemical insecticides.

The lacewing's path to total consumption is not an easy one, however, for aphids have retained the services of a most formidable bodyguard: the ant. The sticky, sweet honeydew that aphids excrete is a foodstuff highly prized by ants, and they will protect aphids fiercely in order to preserve a constant supply of the stuff; acts of hostility towards their 'livestock' are swiftly defended. This is of little consequence, though, to the lacewing, which has found a way to stay a step ahead in the evolutionary arms race, and it's in the most spectacularly macabre way. The larva's soft body is no match for the jaws of an ant; it needs armour, and so it begins to collect material which it attaches to itself. The first material it can procure is its own egg case; this it duly plasters to itself and then hunts for more resources. Aphid exuviae (the 'skins' shed from moulting), plant matter, desiccated bodies of prey – on they all go, woven into a dense, fluffy jacket that make the larva look more like a woolly aphid, or a scale insect, both of which pose no threat to the larva's aphid prey. This grisly Trojan horse can now trundle freely into aphid colonies, picking off individuals with ease. Those long, hollow, curved pincers hook onto the aphid, penetrate the cuticle and suck out the body fluids; a giant pair of straws for feasting on aphid smoothies.

Any 'guardi-ants' that become wise to this wolf in sheep's clothing will attack, only to pull fruitlessly at layer upon layer of detritus and fluff, in which time the aphid lion has time to beat a hasty retreat, back to the dressing-up box.

Giant house spider

Eratigena atrica

EUROPE; LEG SPAN 25–75 mm (1–3 in)

THERE IS A HIGH CHANCE THAT YOU, THE reader, and the house spider have met before. It might have been traumatic. You could have been watching TV and, across the carpet, uninvited, came eight legs with a body attached, seemingly out to get you. Another possibility is that you were just about to run yourself a bath and found that somebody else had got into the tub before you. Again, it was that same uninvited guest, the house spider or – to use its more dramatic name – the giant house spider.

Much is made of the human terror of spiders. Rather less is made of the sheer inconvenience of these unscheduled meetings to the arachnids concerned. You can be perfectly sure that the spider would not have planned to meet a human any time soon. After all, it makes these late-summer and autumn sojourns in search of a mate, and a fall into a bath interrupts those high hopes. Seeing you on its perambulations is a date gone very badly wrong.

Nonetheless, giant house spiders do well in dusty human corners and heated dwellings. There will hardly be any home that doesn't have them, whether in a loft or cellar, or anywhere quiet and neglected. They abound in sheds and outhouses. Most of the time, though, we only see their webs. In contrast to European garden spiders (see pages 156 and 188), which make intricate vertical snares, giant house spiders construct a sheet-web, which is many layers of silk thrown across a space, often near to the ground. There is usually a funnel in the corner that leads to the lair of the owner. These webs can be huge, up to 50 cm (20 in) across. They often look rather ragged and even dusty, so presumably giant house spiders are not enthusiastic housekeepers.

The giant house spider's hunting method is very simple. The web isn't particularly sticky, but the silk threads send an instant message to the owner when something disturbs the surface. This triggers a rapid response, and the spider dashes out to investigate what has happened. If it is prey, the spider deals with it according to size. If the unfortunate prey is small, the web owner simply crushes it to death with its mandibles. If more force is needed (especially for larger prey, such as blowflies and bumblebees), the spider will take a relay of bites and runs, injecting venom into it through a weak point in its exoskeleton. The spider will often retreat at this point and allow the paralyzing effect of the venom to take effect. It will then retrieve the body, bring it to its lair and digest it at leisure. Spiders dose their prey with digestive enzymes and suck the fluid up. At no point does a giant house spider use silk to wrap up its prey.

The life of a giant house spider is quite slow. Females live through the year, and some have been recorded reaching the impressive age of six, so our unloved arachnid tenants could become old friends if we let them.

Females seldom wander from their webs. Each summer or autumn they mate and, in time, produce around 60 spiderlings, which for a month or so live in a semi-social group, before being turfed out to take their chances.

But, of course, in order for that to happen, the male giant house spiders must go wandering. The cool of autumn brings them indoors, making it more likely that spider-human interactions will occur. The male giant house spider has a slimmer abdomen than the female, but its legs are longer, and some may span 75 mm (3 in). They are also, supposedly, the fastest-running spiders on Earth. They have been clocked at 0.53 m/sec (1¾ft/sec), which is 1.9 km/h (1¼mph), presumably over the surface of a carpet. It is not surprising that they are intimidating.

Females live through the year, and some have been recorded reaching the impressive age of six.

The bath encounters are especially unfortunate. The animals simply wander about, fall in and find that their legs don't get enough adhesion to climb out. The slope of a bath is like a mountain for them. Contrary to what many people think, they don't come up from the plughole.

They should be rescued with a glass and paper. Once released, their search for a mate will continue. If all goes well, boy will find girl, and have a tale to tell.

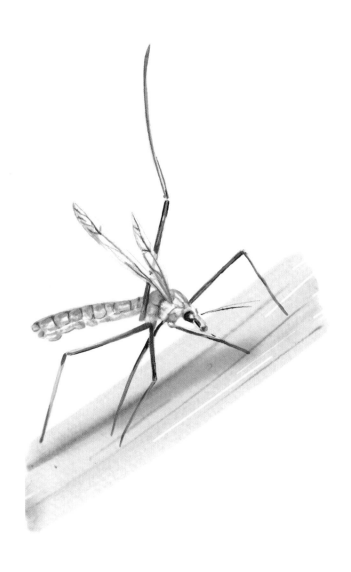

European cranefly

Tipula sp.

EUROPE, ASIA AND INTRODUCED TO NORTH AMERICA;

25–50 mm (1–1¼ in)

IT IS THE SEASON FOR DROPPING LEAVES and, for some insects at least, dropping legs. The word 'deciduous', as used for trees and their foliage, can mean the removal of anything you don't need, and one of the European cranefly's most famous characteristics is the loose connection between its legs and the rest of its body.

Most of us know the European cranefly well, although it is rarely called by that name. In the UK, it is the daddy longlegs, or even granny nobble-knee. In the USA, its similarity to a giant mosquito is reflected in the name mosquito hawk, or even the Texas mosquito – everything is bigger in the Lone Star State. We are accustomed to seeing the cranefly in our gardens, flying with no degree of confidence, often very low over the lawn, legs everywhere, and apparently with almost useless wings. It is an accident-prone insect, continually bumping into things, including lights, to which it is strongly attracted. Life seems difficult for it, as reflected in frequent drowning, squashing and a pitiful end in a spider's web.

It is thought, though, that those extraordinarily long and detachable legs help to reduce the disasters. They might act like cat's whiskers, measuring distance to bumps as the insect moves about, and they might be sacrificed to a predator, including a

It is an accident-prone insect, continually bumping into things.

spider, like the tail of a lizard. They could aid the cumbersome insect to stay balanced, both in flight and on the ground, stabilizing a female when she inserts her ovipositor into the soil. But it is still a curious sight, seeing an animal so completely inured to amputation, going about life as normal.

Despite its likeability, the European cranefly produces some astonishing reactions in people. True, it does have a long rostrum, suggesting that it may bite. It also has a slender body which, in the female, tapers to a sharp-looking ovipositor, which undoubtedly resembles a sting. When craneflies appear in large numbers, as they often do in the early autumn, panic ensues when some disreputable rag warns of a plague of blood-sucking hordes. Yet the truth is that this fly couldn't hurt a fly. It only lives for 10–15 days and many individuals don't eat at all. And it is hardly going to try to lay eggs in your flesh.

Nonetheless the larvae, which have yet another nickname – 'leatherjackets' – can cause a few furrowed brows among humans. These cylindrical, soil-living grubs disgrace themselves by eating the roots, and sometimes the leaves, of grasses, even on well-kept lawns, leaving bare patches. More seriously, they can damage cereal crops.

This is particularly annoying in North America, because two cranefly species – the worst offenders – have been introduced there by accident.

European craneflies, despite their obviously frailties, are among the most successful of all flies, and indeed insects. There are at least 15,000 species in the family, and they include the largest true flies (Diptera) in the world, reaching a wingspan of 110mm (4⅓in). They occur everywhere, including snow at high altitude and the Arctic tundra.

They have also been around a long time, at least since the early Cretaceous (145–66 million years ago), and so they shared the skies with flying reptiles such as pterosaurs and breathed the same air as all our favourite dinosaurs. Indeed, there is a scene in the movie *Jurassic Park* when the scientists attempt to obtain dinosaur DNA from the blood of a 'mosquito' preserved in amber. Says the doyen of fly-lovers Dr Erica McAlister, crossly, in her book *The Secret Life of Flies* (see page 224), 'But the long extraction shot is of an adult cranefly that doesn't even feed, let alone on blood'.

Much-maligned and misunderstood, is the European cranefly. But it carries on anyway.

Large yellow underwing moth

Noctua pronuba

EUROPE, ASIA AND INTRODUCED TO NORTH AMERICA;
WINGSPAN 50–60 mm (2–2⅓ in)

IT'S NOT A GOOD ADVERTISEMENT FOR moth-kind. We've all seen it. A flailing insect, completely bamboozled by something as simple as a lightbulb, flies in ever-decreasing circles and thunders into the lampshade or some other object. It might even flop on to the ground or the wall, only to take off and do the same again. It's not impressive; the optics aren't good.

The moth concerned could be one of many species, but in the late summer and autumn, it's often the ubiquitous large yellow underwing. And if you meet one by day, it may not enhance its reputation. When flushed from the vegetation, it has the same panicky response, apparently zooming off without any thought of where it is going. If you have ever had the joy of being present at the opening of a non-lethal moth-trap, you know that these moths often storm off from the egg boxes, flying into people's faces and generally giving off an excitable, somewhat clueless impression.

But the large yellow underwing is a moth that, at least when it is away from human company, most certainly knows where it is going. Occurring throughout most of Europe and Asia, and introduced into North America, this species is a long-distance migrant. In common with many birds, much admired for their transcontinental journeys, it flies north in summer and south in autumn, for many hundreds of kilometres. While one individual large yellow underwing moth is making a fool of itself in your living room, countless others may be flying over your rooftops some 250–500 m (800–1,600 ft) above the ground, being astonishing.

Welcome to the world of moth migration. Many people have no idea that it happens. Yet so many moths migrate that they can be caught on radar. For example, in central Europe in autumn, multitudes can be seen on screens, while the species involved have been confirmed by moth trapping in the same places on the same nights. It is a significant phenomenon. They leave the area on a south-westerly, heading towards the Mediterranean. They have been measured flying at an average of 15 m/sec (49 ft/sec), or 54 km/h (33½ mph); with a good tailwind they can manage 100 km/h (62 mph). If they fly all night, that is some shift.

This happens on favourable nights in the autumn, while in the spring they go north, aided by south-westerly winds. Nobody knows how many are involved, but maybe there are as many individuals as birds. The individuals flying north breed, and it is their offspring that orient south. This goes far back in the DNA. The DNA is telling them that they must move, and it tells them what direction to take, although nobody knows how. By going south, presumably each individual moth will have the chance to breed in warmer climates.

Their flights beg the question: how do they find their way? They are moths, with small brains and limited eyesight. The chief answer would appear to be a magnetic sense. Researchers placed moths in 'registration cages', which are used for many migration studies. They are round, and a type of paper put around the rim records the moths bumping into the sides. These found that, in autumn, large yellow underwing moths did indeed largely fly south-west. However, when the researchers placed a large electro-magnet under the cage and artificially reversed the polarity, the moths flipped their direction to true north-east – proof that they were using the Earth's magnetic field. In life, moths can maintain their direction by compensating for sidewinds.

Large yellow underwing moths use celestial objects, such as the moon and stars, to find their direction.

There is also some evidence that large yellow underwing moths use celestial objects, such as the moon and stars, to find their direction. At least one study has suggested that the moths use the orientation of stars, apparently those that are 95 degrees away from the Pole Star. There needs to be more research done on this. Birds often use a combination of cues for orientation, including magnetism and stars, so it wouldn't be surprising if insects did too.

So, the next time you see a moth flapping at your lightbulb, remember the artificiality of it all. Put the moth out under the night sky, where it belongs, and wish it on its way.

European garden spider

Araneus diadematus

EUROPE; 9–15 mm (⅓–⅗ in)

AUTUMN SIGNALS MANY CHANGES IN THE natural calendar. Trees, preparing for the winter diapause, suck energy and nutrients from their leaves and down into their roots, creating a change in colour palettes across the landscape. The air cools, not just feeling but *smelling* different. There is a noticeable decline in the number of invertebrates; many have reached the ends of their natural lifespans, and the remainder are hunkering down in preparation to overwinter in a variety of ways, whether it's in a subterranean chamber, wrapped up in a dead leaf or even behind the living-room curtains.

Flying in the face of autumnal inertia, however, is a spider that announces its presence in the most striking fashion. As the mornings become chillier and the dewpoint increases, bejewelled, concentric webs appear *everywhere* around our homes. They are quintessential spider webs, appropriated by all manner of modern cultural references from Halloween décor to Spider Man. The spider responsible for these stunning works of art-chitecture (see what I did there?) is the European garden spider, a master crafter in the construction of these intricate, seemingly perfect circular webs, which are seen by many as the invertebrate harbinger of winter. The webs can vary enormously in size – smaller examples traverse dead plant stems and larger efforts will span across porches and neighbouring buildings, anchored by guy ropes up to over 1 m (3¼ft) in length. You may get into your car on a chilly morning and notice that a thoughtful individual has decorated your car's wing mirror with a pleasing silken adornment.

The European garden spider is one of the orb-weaver spiders (so named for those beautifully round webs) and is also known as the garden cross spider, for more often than not it has a cross-shaped marking on its abdomen. Although somewhat variable in colour, it is an unmistakeable spider. Its base colour ranges from pale to dark, mottled brown, with a darker isosceles triangle down the length of the abdomen, upon which several white markings are arranged together to make the cross shape. The triangle is wider at the base and tapers towards the tip of the abdomen, seemingly pointing to the spinnerets – the tools of the garden spider's trade. It is the spinnerets that produce the high-tensile silk with which the spider constructs the huge webs that seem to appear like magic overnight and glisten in the morning sunlight; many of us have, at some point, walked

As the mornings become chillier and the dewpoint increases, bejewelled, concentric webs appear everywhere.

straight into one as we rush from the house in a bleary-eyed effort to get somewhere on time. A web will appear spontaneously because the spider has worked the night shift on its construction.

The silk of the garden spider is, in fact, three different types of silk, which are liquid until they leave the body, blended and squeezed through nozzles in the spinnerets, and rendered solid, like precision Silly String. A delicate web will sustain irreparable damage from wind, rain, unfortunate prey and clumsy humans, and every couple of days it will need to be completely rebuilt. However, the silk required to build a web is very energy-costly for a spider, and in a neat trick of fuel saving, it will ingest the old web to recycle its properties, and help it to create a new one.

Far from being a cold-blooded killer, the garden spider is a fastidious and protective parent. The female lays a large clutch of eggs, wraps them in a cocoon of her own silk, caches them in a sheltered place, and then guards them in the plummeting temperatures. The eggs remain in dormancy over winter before hatching the following spring. What appears from the egg sac is a mass of tiny, adorable, yellow spiderlings that remain huddled together for protection until they are large enough to venture out and make their way in the world to complete their own life cycles. Relatively few make it to adulthood – many will be eaten or perish, but those who do survive could well be the ones who festoon your garden with diamanté sparkle next autumn.

Peacock jumping spider

Maratus spp.

AUSTRALIA; BODY LENGTH 4–6 mm (³⁄₁₆ in)

ONE OF THE MOST SPECTACULAR SIGHTS IN nature is the courtship dance of the peacock bird. The iridescent, turquoise male lifts and spreads its upper tail feathers in a superb, shimmering fan and shimmies like a samba dancer at Rio Carnival, all in hopes of impressing a female. But what is even more remarkable, is that this exact same behaviour happens in a very different branch of the animal kingdom, in a tiny spider from Eastern Australia.

The peacock jumping spider (*Maratus* spp.) belongs to the Salticidae, which is, in the writer's humble opinion, the cutest family of spiders in the entire world. It has eight eyes, like most spiders, with one huge, convex, primary pair that sit right on the front of the face, giving it the most adorable puppy-dog appearance. These large eyes have free-moving retinas and, combined with the smaller, light-sensitive eyes, contribute to the jumping spider's excellent eyesight. Vision is important to the jumping spider's hunting method; it does not spin a web, instead it uses the stalk and ambush technique. Upon seeing a suitable target, it edges closer to it and then leaps on it so quickly that the unsuspecting prey doesn't stand a chance.

Mating is an equally intrepid exercise and, to maximize its chances, the male peacock jumping spider has evolved a nifty trick or two. To pass on its genes to the next generation, the spider must earn the permission of a female to mate and, to do this, it uses a combination of flashy threads and killer dance moves. Like its bird namesake, courtship begins with a male approaching a female (in the case of the spider, very cautiously); the spider then begins to perform an intricate choreography routine of side-to-side movements, simultaneously vibrating vigorously; the female can literally feel the ground move. It holds aloft its third pair of legs – the ends of which are tipped with white and black hairs for added drama – and then, its *pièce de résistance*: its abdomen pivots up and forwards, extending fringed side panels (known as opisthosomal flaps), in much the same way as a peacock *ahem* 'erects' its feathers. The male's abdomen is covered with tiny, iridescent scales that scatter visible light and create striking blue, green and red colours in species-specific patterns. This creates a stunning halo of iridescent shimmer around the spider's head, which – combined with the flamenco arms and devastating dance moves – would go down a storm on the Sambadrome but is, more crucially, irresistible to females. Well, that's the plan, anyway; females are discerning and will make a potential mate work hard for the honour of siring the next generation. At all points during this lengthy audition (up to an hour), the male is at risk of being eaten. Everything has to be *perfect*: the intensity of the vibrations, the sequence of the sexy semaphore, the butt waving; the entire repertoire has to be absolutely on point. Shoddy wardrobe and lapses in concentration will reap the ultimate consequence. Should everything go as planned, the female will give the male permission to approach her. He climbs (very carefully) on top of his significantly larger partner, rotates her abdomen to reach her epigyne and transfers sperm from his pedipalps. If he's *really* lucky, he will have time to leap quickly to safety. Many males end up being the postcoital meal, which brings a whole new meaning to 'feeding the kids'.

Shoddy wardrobe and lapses in concentration will reap the ultimate consequence.

This remarkable display takes place on a very small scale: peacock jumping spiders measure around 0.5 cm (¼ in) in length and are easy to miss. You may see the females without realizing they are actually peacock jumping spiders, as only the sexually mature males possess the striking iridescent colours. As with peafowl, immature males and female peacock jumping spiders are brown and cryptic; this is often described as 'drab' or 'dull', which sadly undermines the underlying genius of camouflage. Cryptic colouring is as specialized an adaptation as conspicuous markings, with the obvious benefit of improved longevity. It must be worth the risk for males though, to be so conspicuous, as it is the most colourful, distinctly patterned males who win the dance-off and secure their lineage. Get out there in your backyard and have a good look around – it could be full of tiny peacocks all strutting their funky stuff.

WEEK 47

Cape Mounted Rifles bean beetle

Mylabris oculata

SOUTH AFRICA; UP TO 27 mm (1 in)

 SOUTH AFRICA IS HOME TO A HOST OF
magnificent beetles, and few are smarter than the
Cape Mounted Rifles bean beetle, usually called the
CMR bean beetle. It strides across gardens, parks,
scrub and grassland, sporting its very smart livery,
the black with yellow squares resembling the uniform of the long-
disbanded military and police corps of that name.

This is an abundant, large and easily noticed beetle, a forceful
member of the African suburban fauna. 'Forceful' is too polite. This is
an animal not to be messed with. In the course of its life, it can cause
enormous damage to no less than three categories of living things – to
plants, to grasshoppers and to potential predators, including people.

In its range, this beetle is mostly seen on flowers, along with many
other members of the local invertebrate fauna. However, not only does

197

it take pollen, as do the majority, it will also eat foliage and the flowers themselves. And the biggest problem is that, where you get one beetle, you get a lot, because these animals swarm. Their collective effect is to damage plants and impair their growth and, again unfortunately, the CMR bean beetle has generalist tastes. So, not only does it damage many popular garden flowers, it also has a go at crops, conferring upon itself the status of pest. As its name implies, it will go for beans, but also cotton, peaches and various citrus fruits.

While the CMR bean beetle has wide vegetarian tastes, its destruction of grasshoppers is somewhat more pointed and personal. Essentially, the larvae are major predators of the unhappy hoppers. Despite the fact that the adults lay their eggs in the soil, the first stage larvae, as soon as they hatch out, make a bee-line for the egg pods of orthoptera. These first stage larvae are known as triungulins, which sound and look more like an alien race encountered by the crew in *Star Trek* than they do beetle larvae, but they are named for having three hooks on each foot. Grasshopper eggs are their obligate meal, and they can take an enormous toll on them. In fact, in a rare blink of positive news, they can dampen down plagues of locusts.

But of all their remarkable characteristics, CMR bean beetles are best known for their toxicity. When threatened, adults secrete a liquid from their leg joints, a fiery brew indeed. If you hold one of these beetles, your skin will break out in blisters – the CMR bean beetle is in a family, the Meloidae, known colloquially as blister beetles. If you were ever to ingest a beetle by mistake, it would probably kill you. And that's because its body fluids produce a ferociously dangerous toxin known as cantharidin.

'Forceful' is too polite. This is an animal not to be messed with.

Cantharidin is the major component of a folk remedy known as Spanish fly, after a blister beetle found in Europe. For centuries (it is mentioned in Greek literature from the 1st century) it has been taken for various reasons, including as an aphrodisiac. It certainly does cause some stimulation, but anyone taking it is doing the wrong kind of flirting – with death. If you get the quantity wrong, it can easily lead to renal failure and damage to other organs. It is horrible stuff.

Nonetheless, all over Africa, people are still taking CMR bean beetles and grinding them down to a powder. But instead of feeling literally full of beans, the taker beware – it could kill more than your sex drive.

European mantis

Mantis religiosa

EUROPE, ASIA, AFRICA AND INTRODUCED TO NORTH AMERICA;
60–90 mm (2¼–5½ in)

IF EVER A HUNTER ENCAPSULATED THE utter brutality of nature, it would have to be the praying mantis. It is partly its large size and partly its casual demeanour, but there is something garishly cruel about the way that it despatches its flailing invertebrate food. It is an ambush predator, which sits, quietly and concealed within reach of a perch used by potential prey. As soon as something comes near enough, it grabs it with its modified forelimbs, which are often held flexed and together, as if the hunter was supplicating for food. The spines on the legs hold the captured prey – which may be a grasshopper, butterfly or cockroach, for example – in place, and the mantis then simply starts to gobble the nearest piece of flesh, often the head. Spiders at least have the grace to paralyze their prey, and bugs simply insert their needle-like mouthparts and suck out juices. But the praying mantis chews indiscriminately. If it doesn't reach the head at the beginning, it just devours the creature bit by bit, the prey's life ebbing away piecemeal.

The praying mantis is a remarkable insect, which ranges over much of Europe, Africa and Asia, from the warm, dry Mediterranean to the humid tropics, and is frequent in wilder gardens. It has been introduced to North America and is spreading. It is one of about 2,400 species of mantids found in the warmer parts of the world. Many of them have extraordinary camouflage, even resembling flower blossom. Most have a very distinctive triangular head, with huge eyes giving them an alien look. The compound eyes may be composed of some 10,000 ommatidia. Although they have black-and-white vision, they are particularly good at detecting movement. Some vision is overlapping (binocular), making them efficient judges of distance.

Other than their ambush-hunting, praying mantises are probably best known for a quite different game of life and death – sexual cannibalism. The female is larger than the male, and the protracted courtship quite often ends in girl eating boy, the tête-à-tête ending up with just one tête. Somewhat unfortunately, the female sometimes eats the male before he inseminates her, which is either careless or callous, or she does so in mid-coitus, which at least means that the male dies satisfied. There is some evidence that removing the head of the male removes any inhibitions, although it can be difficult to dislodge his stricken body after the deed is done. And plenty of males also die after decoupling.

In this species in the wild, about 31 per cent of encounters end in cannibalism, and by the end of the breeding season, the sex ratio is firmly skewed towards well-fed females. Another study found that male mantises can make up as much as 63 per cent of a female's total diet. Just for good measure, if you keep more than one mantis in captivity, regardless of sex, you will always end up with one – this is the *Hunger Games*, mantis style.

Contrary to what might be inferred, male mantises are not thought to have a self-sacrificial motive, and many can mate with several females. They actively avoid starving females, which they can recognize chemically. If a female has just eaten a male, that's a good sign that she is satiated and well worth the effort. Even so, male mantises must be among the cagiest suitors in the animal kingdom, apart from a few spiders who fear suffering the same fate. The display, if you can call it that, is agonizing, and essentially involves the male creeping up on the female and avoiding that frightening gaze.

The protracted courtship quite often ends in girl eating boy, the tête-à-tête ending up with just one tête.

There is some compensation, even for males that are despatched. A study showed that a female may produce 25 per cent more eggs if she has just dined out on her date. Some of the male's amino acids are directly passed on to the young, bypassing the female's body chemistry.

That's the trouble with investment. It can be risky!

Red postman butterfly

Heliconius erato

AMERICAN TROPICS; 67–80 mm (2½–5¼ in)

THIS REMARKABLE BUTTERFLY IS A COMMON sight in gardens throughout the American tropics. Its long, pointed wings, bright colours and buoyant, flitting flight make it a great favourite as it feeds on flowers in plain sight, taking pollen (not usually nectar) from various blooms, especially the ubiquitous *Lantana*. The odd individual occasionally makes its way further north, wandering as far as Texas.

The red postman is among a group of butterflies known as the Heliconids. Easy to find and breed in captivity, they have been studied by scientists for years, and have helped to reveal how wondrous and complicated tropical ecology can be. This butterfly, in common with most Heliconids, is strongly associated with passion flowers (*Passiflora*), its larval food plant. Caterpillars eat the leaves and, quite obviously, cause damage to any plant that hosts them. Not surprisingly, over the course of evolution, passion flowers, along with many other tropical plants, have evolved chemical defences to curb this intrusion. In the case of passion flowers, they have unleashed a vicious battery of noxious chemicals, such as cyanogenic glycosides and cyanohydrins, which keep just about every herbivorous invertebrate at bay except for the Heliconids. The butterflies have adapted to and even sequestered these dangerous compounds into their body fluids.

It seems that throughout their range, these postmen always ring twice.

One solution for the passion flowers is to prevent the butterflies laying their eggs at all. Some have evolved special nectar-producing organs that look just like Heliconid eggs, 'knowing' that the butterflies prefer not to share egg-laying sites. Others produce super-nectaries, designed specially to attract a raft of super-aggressive ants, bees and wasps, some of them parasitoids of the Heliconids, and to get them suitably drunk on nectar, as if on steroids, and angry. So much for the beauty of the tropics.

The ferocious compounds assimilated into the red postman butterfly's body confer on it the great advantage of being extremely unpalatable to predators. There are hordes of insectivorous birds in the tropics and many of them live longer than your average temperate individual. They learn the patterns of butterflies over time and any experience with an unpalatable meal will mean that they will leave the red postman butterfly alone. In a given location, several unrelated species of butterflies tend to evolve mimicking colours to protect themselves, a red postman butterfly tribute act, if you like – this deceptive, protective similarity is known as Batesian mimicry. The more efficient predators, such as jacamars, have evolved to see through this mimicry, learning to recognize small, giveaway details. More generalized predators are often fooled, though.

However, living in a location with imposters does mean that sometimes the message is lost, and the predator downs a palatable mimic to muddy the waters. In such cases, an even more subtle form of coevolution has arisen. In this case, the unpalatable parties begin to mimic each other, to flood the market with genuinely repellent individuals. This is known as Mullerian mimicry, and the red postman butterfly shows this in spades.

It has coevolved with another, quite different species of Heliconid, known as *Heliconius melpomene*, or the common postman butterfly. What is truly remarkable is that the red postman butterfly has about 20 subspecies, all found in different but distinct parts of its wide range, and each looking somewhat different from one another – it is certainly easy to distinguish them in the field. And amazingly, wherever a distinct red postman butterfly subspecies occurs, there is a corresponding common postman butterfly subspecies, which looks almost identical. It seems that throughout their range, these postmen always ring twice. They are, incidentally, both named scientifically after Greek muses, Erato and Melpomene.

The red postman butterfly has several other unusual behavioural quirks, too. Along with some other Heliconids, it tends to roost communally at night, up in the leaves or tangles, which is very rare among any insects – presumably it is another defensive behaviour. And the males are also somewhat overkeen with mating. Okay, that isn't an exceptional male trait, but what the red postmen do is to find the chrysalis of a female and sit upon it. The moment the female emerges the lothario is on her, and copulation can take place before she has fully emerged. He then places a blob of noxious chemicals on her abdomen to keep other males away.

Greenbottle

Lucilia spp.

WORLDWIDE; BODY LENGTH 10–14 mm (½–⅔ in)

THE AMERICAN POET OGDEN NASH SAID IT succinctly.

'God in his wisdom invented the fly
And then forgot to tell us why.'

This is the attitude most people have towards blowflies (Calliphoridae), of which the greenbottle, still flying around even now, is one. Most people would prefer they didn't exist. They see them as unclean, and plain annoying. Greenbottles are admittedly careless with human personal space, and people kill them for their impertinence. You've almost certainly deliberately swatted one yourself, and there probably isn't any way that we can convince you that they are amazing.

Their gorgeous displays aren't going to convince. No matter that males select fertile females by watching sunlight glint through their wings – and at a precise rate of 178 wingbeats a second. How romantic is that? And no matter that, at the beginning of the display, the male gently head-butts his potential mate, and then constantly taps her body with his forelegs – and that some males are left-legged and some males are right-legged. This still won't convince you.

They are also fantastic pollinators, helping our garden plants and our crops. And if you ever looked at them for more than a second, you might appreciate how very elegantly proportioned they are. And their exoskeletons are bejewelled in lustrous, iridescent, emerald green.

No, this isn't going to work.

But there is no doubt that greenbottles are extremely useful. They can be remarkably beneficial to humankind, so perhaps this could sway the court of public opinion? These humble invertebrates can, believe it or not, be vectors both of justice and healing.

Greenbottles are key organisms in the study of forensic entomology, owing to the fact that they are attracted to dead bodies, including humans, and have a lightning-fast life cycle, one of the quickest of any insects. They are drawn to carrion by smell within 12 hours and immediately lay their eggs. These hatch within a day and can get through three larval stages in 3–4 further days and the pupal stage in another week, depending on temperature. Investigators can work out, simply by greenbottle life cycle development, how long a body has lain in place, which may or may not tally with a suspect's alibi. There will be criminals in jail because they lied and the greenbottles didn't, fuming: 'And I'd have got away with it if it wasn't for you meddling flies!'

But perhaps the biggest debt that people can owe to flies is in the healing of wounds. This is a very ancient practice that has gone through phases of being fashionable, including during the Napoleonic Wars, the American Civil War and the First World War. It is undergoing a resurgence. If you have a wound that needs effective cleaning and healing, medical staff will deliver you greenbottle maggots in a mesh that looks like a teabag. The larval genius is to eat only the dead flesh and the pus and not to damage your living tissue.

These humble invertebrates can, believe it or not, be vectors both of justice and healing.

There are further benefits. The flies produce antibiotic-like substances that keep bacteria in check, and they may even stimulate the growth of new tissue. Larval therapy is safe and effective.

One can still imagine the scenario, though, of a patient undergoing maggot therapy in hospital next to a window on a summer's day. A greenbottle buzzes close by and the patient, unaware of the connection, swats and squashes the insect with a newspaper.

The greenbottle's path to reputational redemption is long and arduous.

Common earwig

Forficula auricularia

EUROPE, WEST ASIA, NORTH AFRICA AND NORTH AMERICA;

13 mm (½ in)

IMAGINE YOU'RE A 'BUG' IN THE INVERT-IVERSE. When it comes to having a relationship with humans, you will fall one of two categories. If you fall into one, you're safe – you'll be loved and revered, and even thought of as cute. This is a rather exclusive camp, occupied primarily by butterflies, bees and dragonflies.

Fall into the other and your destiny is pariah, *ad infinitum*. And why would you fall into the latter camp? No reason whatsoever, but that is the invertebrates' lot. Quite how 99 per cent of insects, spiders and similar arthropods have become *so* loathed and feared by humans is one of the great mysteries of our time, but that is the position in which these unfortunate animals currently find themselves.

Take the common earwig, for example. Small, brown; to all intents and purposes an innocuous creature, but one with the ability to send grown humans screaming for the hills. Why? Because down the centuries it has secured the most terrifying reputation – not to mention name – by way of an urban myth that is at best, dubious and at worst, defamatory. The common earwig is best known to folklore as the beast that crawls into your ear and burrows into your brain. Except it doesn't. There is not one single account of an earwig penetrating the old grey matter. But what of the ear itself? The word 'earwig' comes from the old English *ehre* ('ear') and *wicga* ('beetle', 'insect'). Its scientific name is *Forficula* ('scissors' in Latin) *auricularia* (Latin for 'ear'). The German and Dutch languages also refer to it as an 'earworm'.

Best known to folklore as the beast that crawls into your ear and burrows into your brain. Except it doesn't.

Although there are several anecdotal accounts of earwigs having breached the auricle, and even one scientific paper testifying to such an occurrence, on balance, an earwig is no more likely to enter an orifice that it deems potentially suitable as a roost or nest site accidentally than any other invertebrate and that is an infinitesimally unlikely scenario. I have myself suffered the mass-hysterical misfortune to have an earwig caught in my hair as a child; however, my assumption that it was cynically attempting to gain access to my ear canal was definitely unfounded and based on cultural hearsay. I thought nothing of the poor earwig's unfortunate position, however, as my friends and I screamed and swatted at it with hands and hairclips.

Had I known then what I know now, I would've seen this creature very differently, because would you believe that the earwig has one of the most complex and astonishing wing structures in the entire animal kingdom? Earwigs are a little like beetles, in that they have two pairs of wings: the hindwings are fully formed and used for flight; the forewings have evolved into hard casings (elytra) that protect the hindwings. These elytra are tiny, relative to the size of the earwig's body and so we'd expect the wings to also be very small, right? Oh, no, no, how gloriously wrong we would be! Beneath those teeny casings are gossamer-thin wings that open up like enormous, translucent, rainbowy spinnakers in a downwind. The principle of this 'design' is similar to the way a Spanish *abanico* hand fan opens, around a pivot; the earwig wing goes one step further, with the addition of folding in half to reduce its size even more. Unfolding happens with speed, and we can only observe the phenomenon clearly in extreme slow motion. What we see with our woefully slow human eyes and brains is that the wings pop out like airbags as the earwig launches upwards. Earwigs are thought to possess the largest wing-fold ratio in the known animal kingdom – an expansion of up to ten times their folded size. The wing veins have cunning snap-to joints, which collapse the wing folds rapidly and appear to suck the wings back into the elytra. Research is being undertaken to understand exactly how this feat of physics occurs, and given the issues we humans seem to have even putting a pop-up tent away, we need all the help from earwigs we can get.

Woodlouse

Order Isopoda

WORLDWIDE; 10 mm (½ in)

WE COMPLETE OUR JOURNEY THROUGH A year of bees and bugs with an invertebrate that can be seen in virtually every part of the world on almost every day of the year. A tiny tank whose ubiquity is matched by the sheer quantity of regional names it has accumulated in the British Isles and further afield (over 170, and, just for fun, I will use one from a different county for each mention during this chapter). It is the woodlouse – a creature almost unique in its evolutionary path and, because of it, phenomenally successful. And yet, by virtue of it being neither dangerous to us, nor an object of our affection, the chiggywig (Dorset) is more or less ignored by humans.

The story of the chisel-hog (Kent) began, as with all land animals, in the sea, but evolution eventually drove life onto land, and aquatic arthropods diversified into the more complex insects, spiders and other early arthropods. Monkey peas (Suffolk), however, do not appear to have changed quite so much since their isopod ancestors left the ocean, up to 360 million years ago and are today fully terrestrial crustaceans. *Mochyn coed* (Welsh translation) bear a striking resemblance to the prehistoric trilobites, however they are more closely related to crabs and shrimps. Cheese logs (Berkshire) differ from insects in several ways: rather than having a defined head, thorax and abdomen, they have an exoskeleton made up of articulated sections that provide an armoured 'shell'; underneath this is a soft body with seven pairs of legs. Some species are so flexible that they can curl up entirely. Their eyes are clusters of light-sensitive units called ommatidia, which can vary in number depending on the species. Their eyesight is poor, however, so they use sensitive antennae to help them negotiate their way around in the gloomy recesses of their favoured habitats: damp, dark log piles, compost heaps and other detritus-rich crannies.

Of the many qualities the parson pig (Isle of Man) possesses, one of the most endearing is its parenting methods. The marsupials are widely known as the only animals to carry their young in a pouch, but the humble cheesy-bob (Surrey) also has a secret papoose in which it carries not one, or even several young, but up to *50* fertilized eggs. Most invertebrates lay their eggs on a surface or in a substrate, but mama cudworm (Shropshire) carries them around with her to protect them from predators, even after they hatch. The hatchling sowpigs (Cornwall) that leave the maternal pouch are tiny, soft and pale but soon harden up. The mother continues to tend and guard her progeny; large clusters of what look like family groups can often be found under logs and paving slabs, where youngsters and adults of several different broods intermingle, seemingly cordially.

Billy-buttons (Dorset) are detritivores, meaning they eat dead and decomposing matter, though this can be varied – anything from leaf litter to mould to poo and even cellulose. They process material through their gut and what they expel is then available for smaller animals and bacteria to consume, which is essentially how dead organic matterbecomes compost. For this reason alone, slaters (Dumfries) provide essential recycling assistance to the ecosystem and (along with many other decomposers) prevent us from being up to our eyeballs in waste, a service they perform for free and with such quiet efficiency that we don't even know it's happening.

An invertebrate that can be seen in virtually every part of the world on almost every day of the year.

For such a clandestine creature, the sow-bug (Hertfordshire) has certainly woven its way into our cultural psyche. The variety of names in Britain and Ireland alone is testament to the extent to which the pig louse (Somerset) has captured our imagination. Many of these names are pig-related, the origins of which are so old that the etymology is no longer entirely clear but is said to pertain to the penny-pig's (Essex) resemblance to hogs in a pen. The common rough woodlouse has the scientific name *Porcellio*, which translates from 'porcello', the Latin word for 'piglet'. Pishamares (Norfolk) have even been used medicinally through the centuries; their calcium-carbonate-rich bodies thought to cure indigestion by neutralizing stomach acid. An infusion of carpenters (Newfoundland, Canada) and white wine was prescribed to cure 'chin cough' (now known as whooping cough). Swallowing nine granfers (Avon) daily, washed down with ale, was said to (somewhat ironically) tackle jaundice.

Maybe this explains why they are also called pill bugs ...

Glossary

Abdomen
The rear of the three segments that makes up the body of an insect. Easiest to see in the winged insects. Usually the largest segment and can be patterned or coloured (e.g. yellow and black stripes on social wasps).

Antenna (plural: antennae)
Two appendages that protrude from the head of all insects, and a variety of invertebrates, and function as sensory organs.

Aposematic
Having a brightly coloured or patterned body, to advertise one's toxicity or noxiousness to predators.

Bivoltine
In reproduction, producing two broods per breeding season.

Chitin
A structural polymer found in the exoskeletons of arthropods. Chitin is also a constituent in the cell walls of fungi. One of the most abundant organic compounds on Earth.

Chrysalis
The name given to the pupae of butterflies.

Cocoon
A silken case, spun around the outside of a pupal case, as an extra layer of protection during pupation. Often seen in moths and butterflies. (See also: pupa)

Compound eyes
The visual organ found in arthropods, which is made up of many smaller cells called ommatidia. Sometimes coloured or patterned. (See also: ommatidia)

Crepuscular
Most active in twilight hours, at dusk/dawn.

Cuticle
The outer layer of the exoskeleton, hardened and often waterproof.

Diapause
The interruption of development in an organism to aid survival through adverse conditions (e.g. frost; winter)

Elytra
The modified forewings of beetles, which have evolved into hardened, protective casings. Often colourful, iridescent, or patterned. (See also: forewing)

Exoskeleton
The external skeleton of an arthropod, which protects the soft inner body. It is reinforced with chitin and calcium carbonate.

Exuvia/e
The dried out, moulted outer layer of some invertebrates, such as spiders, cicadas and dragonflies.

Haemolymph
The fluid of the circulatory system of invertebrates. Functions in a similar way to blood, by transporting nutrients, hormones and waste through the body.

Hibernaculum (plural: hibernacula)
A place where animals seek refuge throughout the winter.

Instar
The growth stage of an invertebrate which goes through incomplete metamorphis. Includes true bugs and grasshoppers.

Larva (plural: larvae)
The stage of an insect – which goes through complete metamorphosis – between egg and pupa. (See also: metamorphosis)

Metamorphosis
The complete change from one stage of life to another. Complete metamorphosis: the change from larva to adult through pupation (e.g. beetles, bees). Incomplete metamorphosis: the transformation into adult stage through moulting (e.g. bush-cricket, shieldbug).

Nymph
The pre-adult stage of an invertebrate that undergoes incomplete metamorphosis. (See also: metamorphosis)

Ommatidia (singular: ommatidium)
The individual units – or cells – that make up a compound eye.

Ovipositor
A tube-like egg-laying device in insects. In some insects it is modified for stinging, piercing or sawing.

Parasite
An organism that uses the body of another organism as a food source. The host is not killed. (See also: parasitoid)

Parasitoid
An organism that uses the body of another organism as a food source, usually by laying its eggs within the host's body. The host is eventually killed. (See also: parasite)

Pedipalps
A pair of sensory organs in arthropods, such as spiders, scorpions and crabs. They are located next to the mouthparts, and are often used to grab and hold. In spiders, the pedipalps of the male are enlarged, and are used to transfer sperm to the female.

Polymorphic
Taking two or more different forms, e.g: colour, pattern.

Proboscis
A long, flexible, hollow feeding tube through which nectar or liquid is transported into the digestive tract of an insect.

Pronotum
In insects, the hardened outer layer of the thorax, directly behind the head.

Pupa (plural: pupae)
The hardened cuticle within which certain insect larvae change into adult form. (See also: chrysalis and larvae)

Quiescent
Inactive or dormant

Rostrum
In true bugs (Hemiptera) the long, rigid, hypodermic tube-like mouthparts which pierce plant or animal tissue and suck out the fluids within. In weevils; the elongated 'snout'.

Saproxylic
Living within, and sustained by, dead and dying wood.

Seta (plural: setae)
The stiff, bristle-like hairs that grow out of the cuticle; often functioning as sensory organs to gather information about the surrounding environment.

Spiracles
The small openings on the sides of arthropods which allow transfer of gases such as oxygen and carbon dioxide, as part of respiration.

Thorax
The central section of an insect's body, between the head and the abdomen.

Ventral
The underside of the body.

Index

Further reading

Eaton, Eric R., *Wasps: The Astonishing Diversity of a Misunderstood Insect*, Princeton University Press (2021)

Foitzik, Suzanne and Olaf Fritsche, *Empire of Ants: The Hidden Worlds and Extraordinary Lives of Earth's Tiny Conquerors*, Gaia (2021)

Goulson, Dave, *A Sting in the Tale: My Adventures With Bumblebees*, Vintage (2014)

Jones, Richard, *Ants: The Ultimate Social Insects*, Bloomsbury (2022)

McAlister, Erica, *The Secret Life of Flies*, The Natural History Museum (2018)

Piper, Ross, *How to Read an Insect: A Smart Guide to What Insects Do and Why*, The History Press Ltd. (2021)

Sumner, Seirian, *Endless Forms: The Secret World of Wasps*, William Collins (2022)

Acknowledgements

Grateful thanks to the Batsford team for their hard work in bringing this book to fruition. Huge thanks to Lesley Buckingham for her beautiful illustrations and to Rory Dimond for his superb attention to detail as our entomological consultant. Dominic Couzens would like to thank his long-suffering family, as ever! Gail Ashton would like to thank her family for all their support with her long hours of research and writing.